Paris Monographs in American Archaeology 38

A Sign Catalog: Glyphs in Selected Text-Like Layouts at Teotihuacan

Joanne Michel Guerrero

BAR International Series 2670
2014

Published in 2016 by
BAR Publishing, Oxford

BAR International Series 2670

Paris Monographs in American Archaeology 38
Series Editor: Éric Taladoire

A Sign Catalog: Glyphs in Selected Text-Like Layouts at Teotihuacan

ISBN 978 1 4073 1312 2

© J Michel Guerrero and the Publisher 2014

The author's moral rights under the 1988 UK Copyright,
Designs and Patents Act are hereby expressly asserted.

All rights reserved. No part of this work may be copied, reproduced, stored,
sold, distributed, scanned, saved in any form of digital format or transmitted
in any form digitally, without the written permission of the Publisher.

BAR Publishing is the trading name of British Archaeological Reports (Oxford) Ltd.
British Archaeological Reports was first incorporated in 1974 to publish the BAR
Series, International and British. In 1992 Hadrian Books Ltd became part of the BAR
group. This volume was originally published by Archaeopress in conjunction with
British Archaeological Reports (Oxford) Ltd / Hadrian Books Ltd, the Series principal
publisher, in 2014. This present volume is published by BAR Publishing, 2016.

Printed in England

BAR titles are available from:

	BAR Publishing
	122 Banbury Rd, Oxford, OX2 7BP, UK
EMAIL	info@barpublishing.com
PHONE	+44 (0)1865 310431
FAX	+44 (0)1865 316916
	www.barpublishing.com

For my parents, Donald and Antonia Michel

Preface

The goal of this study was to yield a closer examination and catalog a limited set of glyphic elements found at the archaeological site of Teotihuacan in Mexico. This study serves as an initial investigation to verify whether these glyphs may be part of a writing system in use at the site. I chose to look at two specific sources of glyphs and glyph compounds at Teotihuacan that appear to be the largest sets of co-occurring glyphs and contain the largest number of glyphs. One set, in particular, has not yet been studied in detail and therefore will present new information within this area of research. Furthermore, there has not been a steady or significant amount of glyphic research carried out at Teotihuacan in recent years, since Taube (2000).

The investigation was structured to thoroughly analyze the data for similarities between the selected glyphic elements from Teotihuacan and the requirements for writing systems. For that reason, I conducted basic linguistic tests on the data to determine whether the glyphic elements had similarities with those requirements for Mesoamerican writing systems.

This work is not a decipherment. Instead, its aim was to verify whether the glyphic elements at Teotihuacan could potentially be a writing system, catalog them in an orderly fashion, conduct a comparative analysis between them and others found within Teotihuacan and elsewhere in Mesoamerica, and conclude whether further research in the way of a complete decipherment is a possibility if future data is uncovered at the site.

Acknowledgements

First and foremost, I want to thank Terrence Kaufman who has been my mentor and great friend for many years. In my opinion, he is without a doubt the most knowledgeable scholar of Mesoamerican Linguistics, and I have been privileged to work closely with him throughout the years in both Linguistics and Anthropology. Without his constant support, collaboration, assistance and encouragement, I would not be the person that I am today.

Additionally, I am thankful to Rubén Cabrera Castro, for without his initial work at La Ventilla in the 1990's, this project would not have been possible. He was very gracious to host me at the site of Teotihuacan so that I could view the Plaza Glyphs for myself, which was extremely important to me. Although it was technically not necessary to see the glyphs in person in order to carry out a study of this kind, it was meaningful for me to see them and made my research for this study much more personal.

I am very appreciative to Brian Stross who has been not only a friend, but provided me with support, inspiration and many helpful suggestions over the years. Also, I would like to extend sincere thanks to Karl Taube who has been so kind as to keep in touch with me over the years, offer insight and to look over my work.

I want to give special thanks to Eric Taladoire for his editorial help and suggestions in the final preparations of this document. It was a privilege for me to have him review my work. Also, I want to acknowledge David Davison for his guidance and assistance in bringing this work to publication with the BAR International Series.

Finally, I really want to thank my family for their constant encouragement. I am more than grateful to my dad and mom, Donald and Antonia Michel, for their loving support, help and confidence in my abilities. They have been there for me through it all and have never questioned my choices for my academic career. They have always stood behind me and my decisions.

Last, but certainly not least, it is impossible for me to thank my husband, Luis Guerrero, enough for his care and patience with me and my research. It takes a very special person to manage being married to an anthropologist. He has graciously spent thirteen years and counting assisting me in Mexico at remote archaeological sites, in the middle of the jungle and in small indigenous villages. He is one of very few people who truly understand my passion for *all things* Mesoamerican.

Contents

Preface I

Acknowledgements II

Contents III

Illustrations IV

Historical Background 1

Writing Systems 5

The Wagner Murals 9

The Language of Teotihuacan 13

Decipherment 15

Methodology 16

Comparative Analysis 21

Speech and Sound Scrolls 37

Readable Glyphs 43

Readable Glyphs 53

Unreadable and partially-eroded glyphs 61

Glyph Compounds 62

Boundary Markers and/or Divider Glyphs 63

La Ventilla/Mural Painting Comparative Analysis 64

Mesoamerican Day Names 66

The Twenty Mesoamerican Day Names from the 365-day Calendar 67

Conclusions 68

Bibliography 72

Illustrations

Figure 1. Map of Mesoamerica. 1

Figure 2. Map of Central Mexico with select archaeological sites. 2

Figure 3. Plan of the Central Zone of Teotihuacan.. 3

Figure 4. Teotihuacan chronology (ceramic)... 4

Figure 5. Teotihuacan style talud/tablero architecture. 4

Figure 6. Logogram for 'earth' from Xochicalco, Morelos... 7

Figure 7. Ways of writing linguistic elements 7

Figure 8. Glyph variants from flowering trees found in the Wagner Murals.. 9

Figure 9. Wagner Mural Collection; Serpent I. 10

Figure 10. Wagner Mural Collection; Serpent I... 11

Figure 11. Glyph compounds from flowering trees found in the Wagner Murals................................ 12

Figure 12. Glyph compound from La Ventilla, Teotihuacan. 17

Figure 13. Glyph compounds of verbs with syllabic signs... 17

Figure 14. Glyph compound of a Maya Personal Name. 17

Figure 15. Glyph compounds that are Aztec toponyms.. 18

Figure 16. Calendric element referent of a personal name.. 18

Figure 17. Mesoamerican Year-Bearer glyph from Xochicalco, Morelos.. 18

Figure 18. Mayan glyph that encodes a noun.. 18

Figure 19. Mayan writing. Clause from the text on Yaxchilan Stela 12.. 19

Figure 20. "TWISTED ROOT" glyph variants in Mesoamerica.. 21

Figure 21. Possible "BUNDLE" variants at Teotihuacan... 21

Figure 22. Teotihuacan style glyphs found at Monte Alban from the *Lápida de Bazán*. 22

Figure 23. Teotihuacan style glyphs found at Xochicalco, Central Mexico... 23

Figure 24. LV glyphs with similar style glyphs from Xochicalco.. 24

Figure 25. Teotihuacan style glyphs in Vera Cruz, Piedra Labrada 24

Figure 26. Stela triad, Xochicalco 25

Figure 27. Teotihuacan style glyphs found at Xochicalco. 26

Figure 28. Teotihuacan style glyphs found on Olmec monuments and reliefs.. 26

Figure 29. Select Teotihuacan style glyphs found in Aztec Codices. 27

Figure 30. FOOTPRINT Glyphs 28

Figure 31. MAGUEY SPINE Glyphs 29

Figure 32. DEER-SNAKE Glyphs. 30

Figure 33. Mural painting of Tlalocan, Tepantitla, Teotihuacan. 31

Figure 34. Mural paintings found near the Palace of the Sun. 32

Figure 35. REPTILE EYE Glyphs 33

Figure 36. QUINCROSS Glyphs. 33

Figure 37. FLAME Glyphs. 34

Figure 38. MOUNTAIN variant Glyphs. 35

Figure 39. Glyph Clusters 35

Figure 40. WATER MONSTER Glyphs 36

Figure 41. Speech Scrolls with glyphic elements in Mesoamerica. 38

Figure 42. Speech Scrolls from Tepantitla, Teotihuacan with glyphic elements.. 39

Figure 43. Glyphic Elements attached to or found inside of speech scrolls. 40

Figure 44. Numerical coefficients with glyphic elements at Teotihuacan. 66

Figure 45. LV glyphs that resemble day names in other Mesoamerican writing systems. 67

Figure 46. Linear texts at LV. 69

Figure 47. Xochicalco Logographic Writing from the Stela Triad. 70

Historical Background

The great Classic period metropolis of Teotihuacan, in my opinion, is of the most fascinating Mesoamerican archaeological sites. Mesoamerica (middle America), as a geographical, cultural and linguistic area, includes the southern two thirds of Mexico, Guatemala, Belize, El Salvador and parts of Honduras, Nicaragua and Costa Rica.

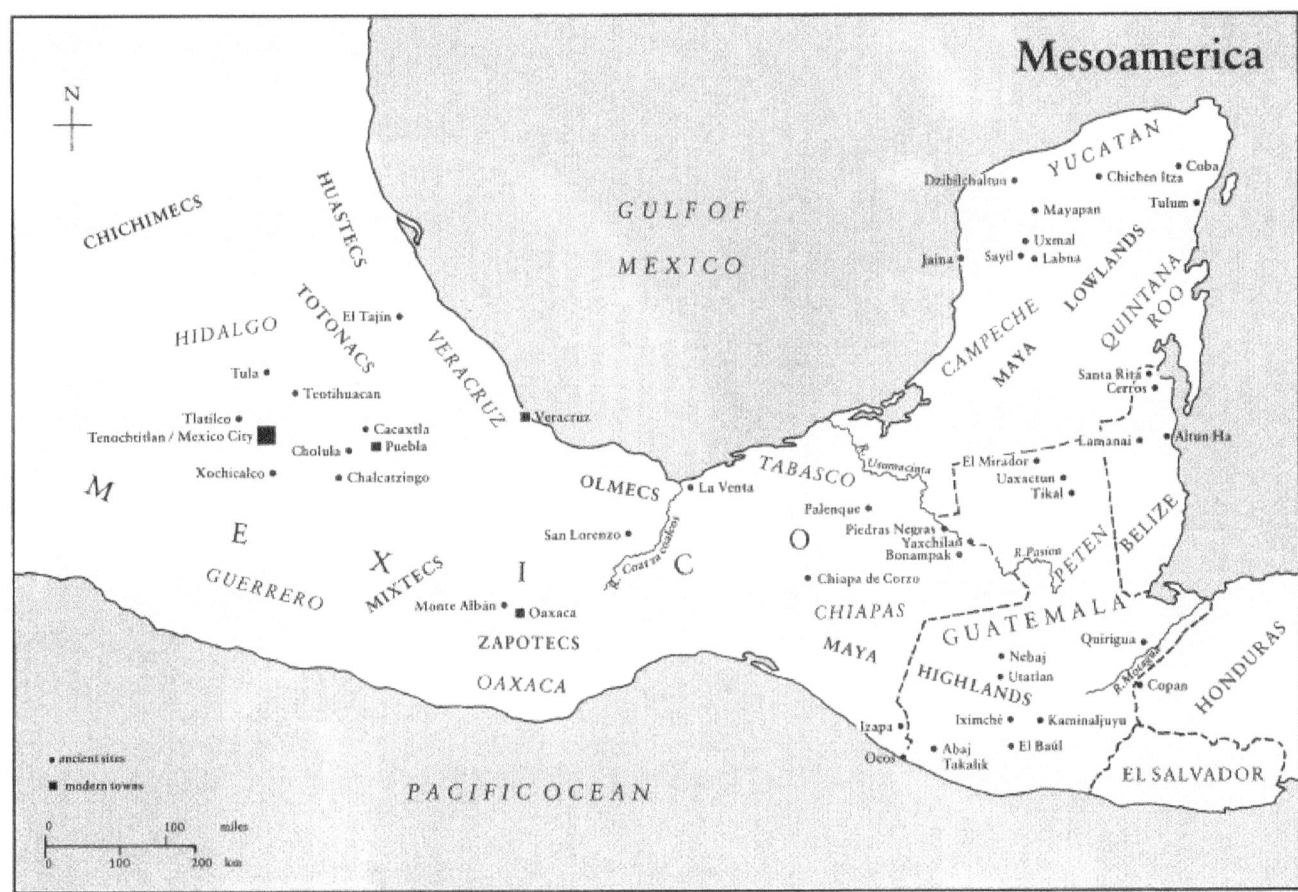

Figure 1. Map of Mesoamerica from Taube 1993: 6.

A detailed list of specific cultural traits that define Mesoamerica was established by Paul Kirchoff in 1943, and is still accepted today by most scholars. Some of these traits included lake gardens (*chinampas*), cultivation of cacao, a certain type of digging stick, architecture including step pyramids, calendars of 18 months of 20 days plus 5 additional days, ball courts with rings, good and bad omen days, pyrite mirrors, stucco floors, sandals with heels, the flying game (*juego del volador*), cultivation of maguey, and the grinding of corn softened with lime or ashes. Mesoamerica owes its distinctive traits to the early domestication in or around the Tehuacan valley (central Mexico) and other areas (Oaxaca, for instance) of maize, beans, and other cultigens (as much as 7000 years ago) (Kaufman 1994: 34).

The archaeological site of Teotihuacan is situated in the Basin of Mexico some 50km to the northeast of Mexico City, and the city is located on the lower slope of Cerro Gordo, an eroded volcanic cone (Evans and Berlo 1992: 8). Some other archaeological sites of importance in Central Mexico include Xochicalco, Tula and Tenochtitlan. Xochicalco is located about 120km (75 miles) south of Mexico City in the state of Morelos and was occupied during the late Classic period (700-

900 CE) after the decline of Teotihuacan (Hirth 2000). Tula (*Tollan*) is located approximately 80km (50 miles) north of Mexico City and was the capital of the Toltec state from the Late Classic to Early Postclassic period (750-1200 CE) (Cobean 2013). Tenochtitlan is located in Mexico City and was the capital of the Aztec polity. It was founded in the late Postclassic period (1325 CE) (Mendoza 2001).

Figure 2. Map of Central Mexico with select archaeological sites. After Taube (2000) map 1.

The Teotihuacan culture occupied the time period of roughly 100 CE - 600 CE, although many scholars will argue it dates back as far as 150 BCE. The entire city was laid-out in a highly systematic and organized grid-like pattern. The ceremonial center alone measures roughly 3km by 1.5km, though it is speculated that in its heyday, this site covered more than 20km and housed well over 150,000 to 200,000 inhabitants. Teotihuacan is generally considered uncharacteristic compared to other Mesoamerican civilizations because the city contained a series of apartment compounds. All the same, we must not forget that the city grid fits with the same symbolic pattern that is found in most Mesoamerican cities.

The inhabitants of Teotihuacan, referred to as the Teotihuacanos, were a group of people who behaved in a manner atypical of other Mesoamerican civilizations. Unlike their neighbors, the Zapotecs of Oaxaca and the Mayas of southern Mesoamerica, the Teotihuacanos placed little emphasis on documenting history through writing. This is perplexing, because based on nothing more than the sheer size of Teotihuacan, one would expect the need for some system of record-keeping.

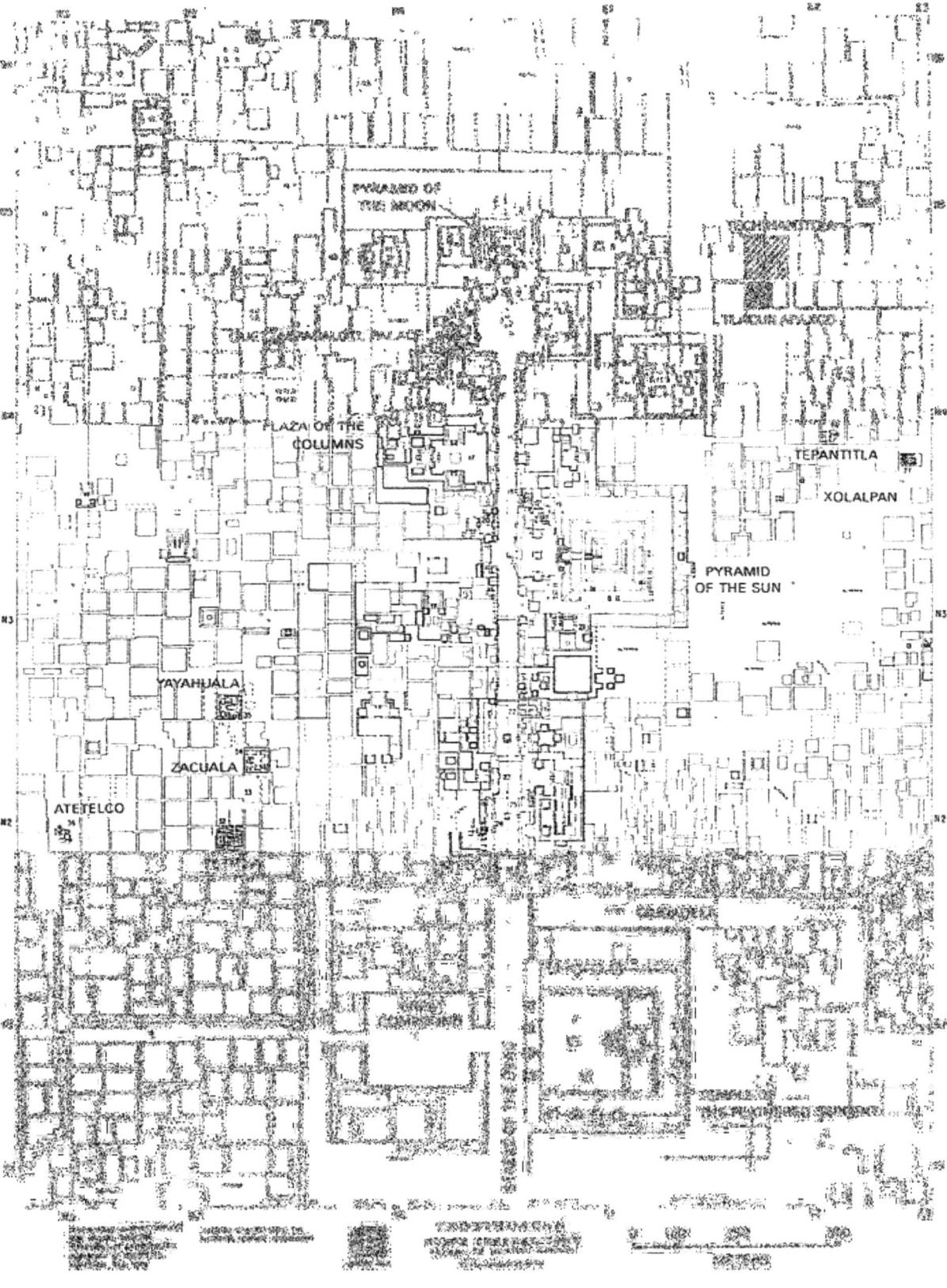

Figure 3. Plan of the Central Zone of Teotihuacan. After Rene Millon, ©1968

Patlachique	BCE 150 – 0 CE
Tzacualli	CE 1 – 150
Miccaotli	CE 150 – 200
Tlamimilolpa	CE 200 – 350
Xolalpan	CE 350 – 550
Metepec	CE 550 – 650

Figure 4. Teotihuacan chronology (ceramic). After Cowgill 1997: Figure 1.

The seemingly deliberate absence of a written language at Teotihuacan is perhaps the most notable difference between it and other Mesoamerican civilizations. The Mayans and Zapotecs left behind highly developed systems of hieroglyphic writing carved on stone stela and recorded in painted books(both written and pictorial). By contrast, no similar carved inscriptions or documents have been found at Teotihuacan. The Teotihuacanos did however leave behind an abundance of mural paintings, art and iconography. The ethnic identity of the Teotihuacanos has long been assumed to be merely an earlier version of Aztec culture (Pasztory 1997: 13). Kaufman (2001b) and Chadwick (2013) have both studied this theme in detail.

Teotihuacan architecture is noted for its *talud/tablero* architectural style. This style of pyramid, with the sloping *talud* and vertical *tablero,* is one of the most salient features of Teotihuacan architecture. When *talud/tablero* architecture is found in other Mesoamerican archaeological sites, such as Kaminaljuyú in Guatemala or Tingambato in Michoacan, Mexico, they are sometimes referred to as being constructed in *Teotihuacan*-style architecture in addition to *talud/tablero* style.

Figure 5. Teotihuacan style talud/tablero architecture; after Gendrop 1984.

Teotihuacan was named the *birth-place* of the gods by the Mexica-Tenochca (better known as the Aztec). In Fray Bernardino de Sahagún's life's work now referred to as the *Florentine Codex*, it is written that the gods gathered in Teotihuacan to create the sun and the moon. According to one source, Motecuhzoma Xocoyotzin (the last Aztec ruler) went to perform rites at Teotihuacan every twenty days. In addition, Aztec-style sculptures have been found near the Pyramid of the Sun, supporting the idea that it was a shrine for the Aztecs (López Luján 1989). For these and numerous other reasons, scholars wish to compare the Teotihuacanos to the Aztecs; however, the differences between the two are many.

Writing Systems

Writing systems throughout history have both fascinated and challenged scholars. One highly debatable question surrounding writing is how to define it. "Almost all the scholars who have looked seriously at writing systems in their general sense have defined writing as spoken language that is recorded or referenced phonetically by visible marks" (Boone 1994: 5). Linguist I.J. Gelb believes, "Those general linguists (that allow for non-phonetic components to writing) who define writing as a device for recording speech by means of visible marks, and take the written to be a point-by-point equivalent of its spoken counterpart, show little appreciation of the historical development of writing and fail to see that such a definition cannot be applied to its early stages, in which writing only loosely expressed the spoken language" (Gelb 1952: 11). Gelb, a scholar of Old World writing, defines writing as "a system of human intercommunication by means of conventional visible marks" (Gelb 1952: 12).

The earliest form of notation is pictographic. Pictography represents ideas or objects with a picture. Pictography itself is not a writing system, though early forms of writing evolved out of pictographic representations. These drawings attempt to communicate a certain message by certain persons in a way that could be understood by the people for whom the message was intended. They do not serve the purpose of pictures in the normal sense since they were drawn for the purpose of communication and not for the purpose of artistic-aesthetic expression (Gelb 1952: 34-35). All Mesoamerican scripts have their basis in pictographic images and vary in their ability to encode complex data(Berlo 1989: 20). Gelb considers pictography a descriptive or representational stage of the forerunners of writing (Gelb 1952: 36). Some scholars try to find ways of accepting pictography as a form of writing but others are highly opposed to this. John DeFrancis, an American Linguist, has written:

> The forthright answer to how pictographs work as a system is that they don't. Pictographic writing is not a system. It is at best exceedingly limited in what it can express and who is able to understand it ... And it should not be called writing without the clearly expressed reservation that it refers to a very restricted type of communication ... While it may be legitimate to discuss pictography in a comprehensive study of human communication, to include them in works devoted to writing only obscures the issue unless they are clearly and categorically dismissed as limited, dead-end means of communication (DeFrancis 1989: 47, 57).

The American Art Historian Janet C. Berlo believes, "It may be that a Eurocentric definition of writing as separate from image-making accounts for the low opinion that many Old World epigraphers have of the Mesoamerican systems; leading scholars of Old World writing routinely disparage Mesoamerican writing systems and deny them credit as full writing systems" (Berlo 1989: 19). Berlo also suggests that the concept of "embedded text" explains the relationship of Mesoamerican texts and images (Berlo 1983: 11-17). She explains that in an embedded text, linguistic content is embedded within the image; art does double duty as logogram and picture (Berlo 1989: 19). The American Art Historian George Kubler, a pioneer in the study of Teotihuacan writing, characterized the art of Teotihuacan as,"less interested in recording appearances than in combining and compounding associative meanings in a quest for viable forms of writing"(Kubler 1967: 5).

All writing systems evolve out of an iconographic system. Iconography is a form of visual art that can be confused with writing. Iconography, in general, is the set of visual symbols manipulated by a culture from a specific part of the world. These visual symbols, when combined or grouped together in one specific area, form a system that is referred to as an iconographic system.

Generally, iconographic symbols do not fall within a narrow range of sizes; they can be both big and small. It is laid out with some constraints, but these are different from those of a writing system. The symbols appear freer and more variable. Usually, there are not as many iconographic elements as there are signs in a writing system.

In the case of Teotihuacan, iconographic interpretation has been a rich source of hypotheses about the religious beliefs, political and social structure and external relations (Langley 1986:5). Clara Millon, an archaeologist well known for her work on the mural paintings of Teotihuacan, and recognized as an expert on Teotihuacan art, has written:

> No knowledgeable student of Teotihuacan art and artifacts has doubted that the Teotihuacanos had evolved a system of signs. But ... it has been much more difficult to sort out what rules the Teotihuacanos did observe in forming and ordering their signs... Our extant legacy consists of a very partial lexicon (one which I believe has been grossly underestimated quantitatively) and virtually no knowledge of whatever syntactic structure may have been employed. Just as important, we do not know the rules governing usage and placement of glyphs (Millon 1973: 306).

The iconographic traits exhibited in texts will be culture specific and a good ethno-historical background of the civilization whose writing system is to be studied is essential to an overall understanding of the meaning of the glyphs.

In 1899, Isaac Taylor presented a five-stage sequence for the development of writing, which he explained as a progression from pictures to pictorial symbols, verbal signs, syllabic signs, and ultimately alphabetic signs (Taylor 1899, 1: 5-6). A salient feature of writing is that it has a format. Terrence Kaufman and John Justeson in an unpublished work on Zapotec hieroglyphic writing in 2001, have described this format with the following criteria: 1) sign shapes of roughly the same width and no higher than wide, 2) reading format, which involves layout, sign orientation, principles of sign combination and reading order. The layout should be in rows or columns; the sign orientation is such that the front ends face the direction one reads from; principles of sign combination may be stacked, side-by-side, attached/affixed and reading order in columns is top down or bottom up and in rows left-to-right, right-to-left and boustrophedon. The difficulty lies in decoding the format being used by the system to be deciphered.

Some scholars believe that the aforementioned criteria for writing systems cannot apply cross-culturally or in all situations. In Mesoamerica, there is a close association between writing (text) and art. Some fully developed phonetic writing systems which have been deciphered, such as the Maya script, have an extremely aesthetic value. Although Maya writing does follow a linear format, it is possible that not all Mesoamerican systems will do so. Perhaps a defining characteristic or criteria of some Mesoamerican writing is expressing an aesthetic value in addition to having a linear format. Trying to force the rich and varied manifestations of Teotihuacan logograms and symbols into a linear pattern of texts seems fundamentally misguided; the search for linear texts at Teotihuacan imposes a Western-style notion of writing upon a vastly different communication system (Berlo 1989: 21). For these reasons, I believe that Teotihuacan iconography and signs should not simply be dismissed because it *appears* on the surface that they do not follow a linear format. They may in fact have a unique format that only those who wrote the texts were privy to understanding. Every aspect of probable Teotihuacan writing deserves our attention; not just those texts that follow a limited set of constraints used elsewhere.

Fully developed writing systems are characterized by employing signs with the ability to (a) represent words; (b) spell out syllables; or (c) spell out sounds. There are three main types of Full Writing Systems and these are Logographic, Logo-syllabic, and Phonetic. Logographic systems contain no phonetic elements and only reveal linguistic structure through word order. Logograms are characters in writing which represent a word or lexeme as a whole (Fig. 6), as the signs 4 (four) and $ (dollar).

Figure 6. Logogram for 'earth' from Xochicalco, Morelos. After Kaufman and Justeson 1998.

There is no doubt that widely understood logograms were an important aspect of visual communication at Teotihuacan (Berlo 1989: 20). Logo-syllabic systems contain both logograms and phonetic signs, or phonograms. Phonograms are written entities that represent a particular sound or syllable. There are two types of phonograms. One type is a Syllabogram that is a phonogram that represents a syllable. The other type is an Alphabetic sign or letter, a symbol that represents a sound. Phonetic writing systems use their set of signs to spell out a string of the syllables or sounds of the words in a language. For a particular set of symbols to be accepted as a writing system, it must be shown that it contains signs of one or more of these types, and that they can be shown to express messages in particular languages.

The ways of writing the linguistic elements of these three systems is detailed below (Fig. 7). In all cases, the signs when combined form a system. The figure details what type of sign we use when we want to represent a particular linguistic entity, and what we call the system of these signs.

	Written Sign	System of Signs
Phoneme	Alphabetic Sign or Letter	Alphabetic Writing or Alphabet
Syllable	Syllabic Sign or Syllabogram	Syllabic Writing or Syllabery
Word	Logogram or Word Sign	Logography or Word Writing

Figure 7. Ways of writing linguistic elements, After Gelb 1963: fig. 2

History of Research on Teotihuacan Writing and Mesoamerican Glyph Interpretation

Although the study of Teotihuacan writing is not an area of research with a large number of dedicated investigators, a number of scholars have experimented with it. Eduard Seler developed the first methods for iconographic interpretation in Mesoamerica in the late 19th and early 20th centuries with his 1904 work on Mexican Picture Writing. James Langley, in the 1980's, conducted a detailed study of what he calls symbolic notation (1986), and several other scholars including Alfonso Caso(1967), Kubler (1967) and Esther Pasztory (1988–93) looked in great detail at the mural paintings. Beginning in the 1990's, Karl Taube looked at the possibilities of a writing system at Teotihuacan (2000). I believe that Taube has made a major contribution with his work in this area. "The study of Teotihuacan writing is still in its infancy, with a great deal of basic identification and documentation of the glyphic signs remaining to be performed" (Taube 2000: 48). Taube concluded that what is present at Teotihuacan is writing. He states that the glyphic elements found at Teotihuacan do in fact comprise a complex system of hieroglyphic writing (Taube 2000: 2). I also believe there to be sufficient evidence that there was a type of writing system employed at Teotihuacan, even if it is unclear specifically what type it was as of now. However, I do not feel that all of the signs found at Teotihuacan are from a particular writing system. The most likely scenario is that some signs are writing, while others are iconography.

While many scholars have looked at Mesoamerican sign interpretation, the first to tackle the Mesoamerican writing system methodically was Eduard Seler (1904). His work was exceptional because he developed the first coherent interpretation of the iconography of sixteenth-century codices, which is still the "unquestioned canonical approach for most of those who write on Mesoamerican iconography" (Pasztory 1997: 64). The Selerian approach even today still is thought to comprise the basic steps for iconographic research. In short, the Selerian method suggests to: 1) "use the largest possible sample of material to analyze; 2) describe forms carefully; and, 3) compare objects for similarity of form and symbolic usage" (Evans and Berlo 1992:16). Seler believed that a similarity in meaning would lead to formal similarity. His type of "ethnographic analogy" or "direct historic approach", postulates that the study of late Mexican manuscripts provides a great deal of ethnographic data that could prove useful in clarifying the meaning of earlier material (Evans and Berlo 1992: 16). Although Seler used Mexican/Aztec manuscripts in his studies, he did not accept a direct line of continuity between Teotihuacan and the Mexica.

Some other scholars have tried to break away from the Selerian approach. Erwin Panofsky, an art historian, in his 1939 work entitled *Studies in Iconology*, believes that "one uncovers the meaning of a work of art through the study of the art itself, as well as through inquiry into the historical character of a specific place and point in time" (Evans and Berlo 1992: 17). In continuity with Panofsky, George Kubler (1967) has rejected the use of analogy all together and feels that the direct analysis of objects within their own era is the best method, and he also completely rejects any use of Aztec sources. I believe that Karl Taube has the best method, and it is the one that I also applied in my study. The use of a far ranging comparative analysis from earlier times to later times seems to be the most efficient. This way, all data are examined and nothing is left out. Esther Pasztory, an art historian, assumes that art reflects culture. This assumption will be used in this study as well. Even in a linguistic study, it is crucial to understand that much of what is present at Teotihuacan is art. Having a command of this style of art and an understanding of the interpretation of it is not only advantageous, but necessary. The glyphs found at Teotihuacan pose a difficult problem with reference to interpretation. Teotihuacan art does, at its core, share some characteristics with that of the Olmecs, Mayas and Aztecs. However, Teotihuacan art is more difficult because the contexts are "less naturalistic and narrative" (Pasztory 1997: 62).

The Wagner Murals

The Wagner Murals are a collection of 70 mural fragments bequeathed to the Fine Arts Museum of San Francisco by the late Harold Wagner, who was an art enthusiast. Although not cataloged in this work, the Wagner Murals should be mentioned when discussing Teotihuacan writing (Berrin, Millon *et al.* 1988).

The mural fragments range in size from a few inches to fourteen feet, they date from between 400–600 CE, and the subject matter of the murals range from elaborate priest deities in warrior-like costumes to large birds and feathered serpents flanked by flowering trees (Bone 1986: 2-7). The "feathered serpents and flowering trees with glyphs" collection proves most valuable to those interested in Teotihuacan writing. The mural called Serpent I (Fig. 9 & 10), with its complete set of thirteen trees and remarkably well-preserved color is of particular interest. Some scholars believe that the flowering trees with glyph compounds may function as toponyms.

Pasztory states, "One of the most beautiful rooms in Teotihuacan must have been the one with feathered serpents painted on a *tablero* above a small *talud* with flowering plants with glyphs" (Berrin *et al.* 1988: 137). These mural fragments are not only very important to the study of Teotihuacan art, but also writing. This collection consists of four separate serpent murals positioned above varying numbers of flowering trees. At least nine different compounds with glyphic elements consisting of as many as three and four separate signs are painted in the trunk of each tree (Berrin *et al.* 1988: 137). There are variations of the different glyph compounds found in association with each of the four different serpent murals.

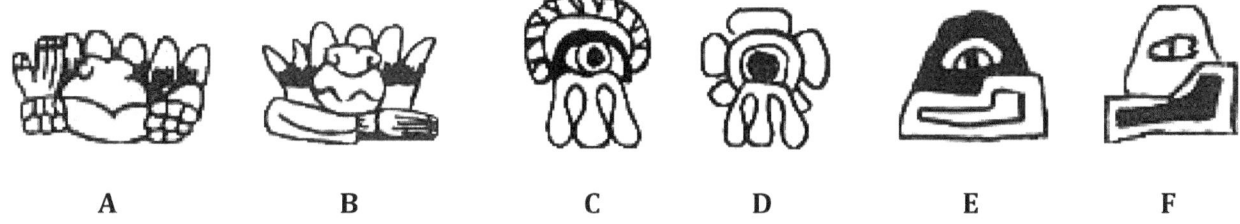

Figure 8. Glyph variants from flowering trees found in the Wagner Murals (a-e) Serpent I, (f) Serpent II. After Berrin *et al.* 1988: fig. VI.3-6.

The roots of the flowering trees, which are twisted, leave room for interpretation that the trees serve a locative function (Fig. 11). In other Mesoamerican writing and pictographic systems, twisted roots indicate place names. The roots of a tree are bound to the earth in a fixed position therefore they can indicate that a place is "fixed", such as a city or important geographic location (mountain, cave, lake). Without a detailed study of the Wagner Mural glyph compounds in association with their positions in the murals, it is not possible to determine that they in fact function linguistically as locatives. It seems a probable hypothesis to form that the glyph compounds are place names given their association with trees and roots. However, given some of the compounds contain as many as three or four different glyphic elements, they could also be phonetic signs that spell out words. In the case of the latter, a larger body of data than what we presently have uncovered would be necessary to conduct further linguistic testing.

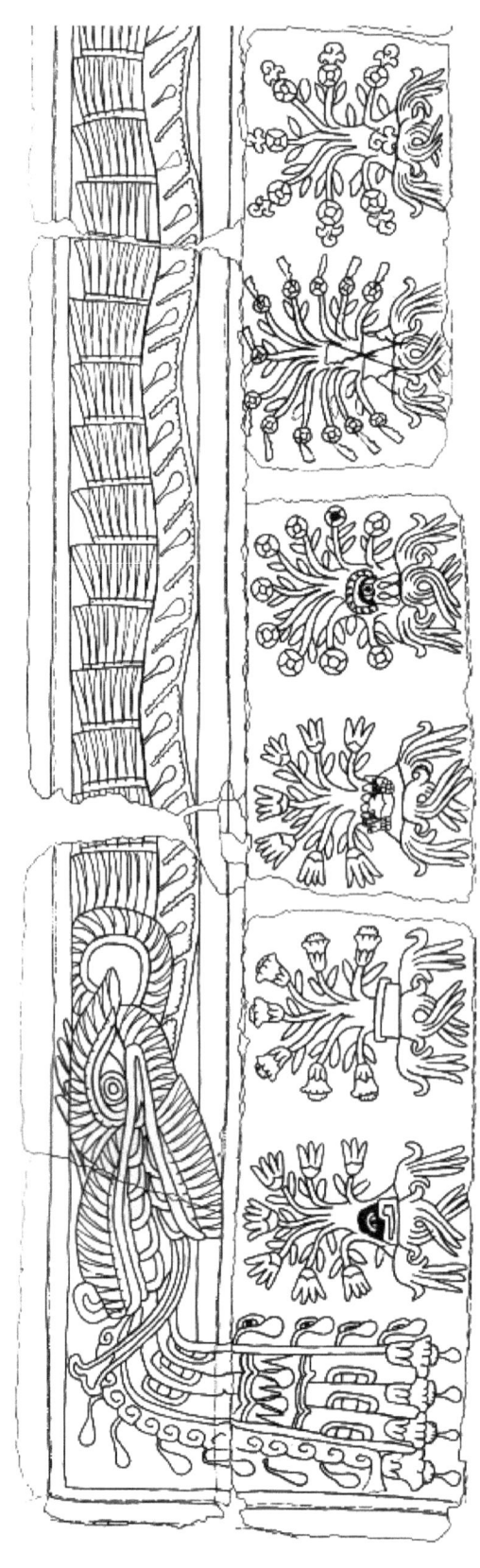

Figure 9. Wagner Mural Collection; Serpent I. After Berrin *et al.* 1988: Fig.VI.1

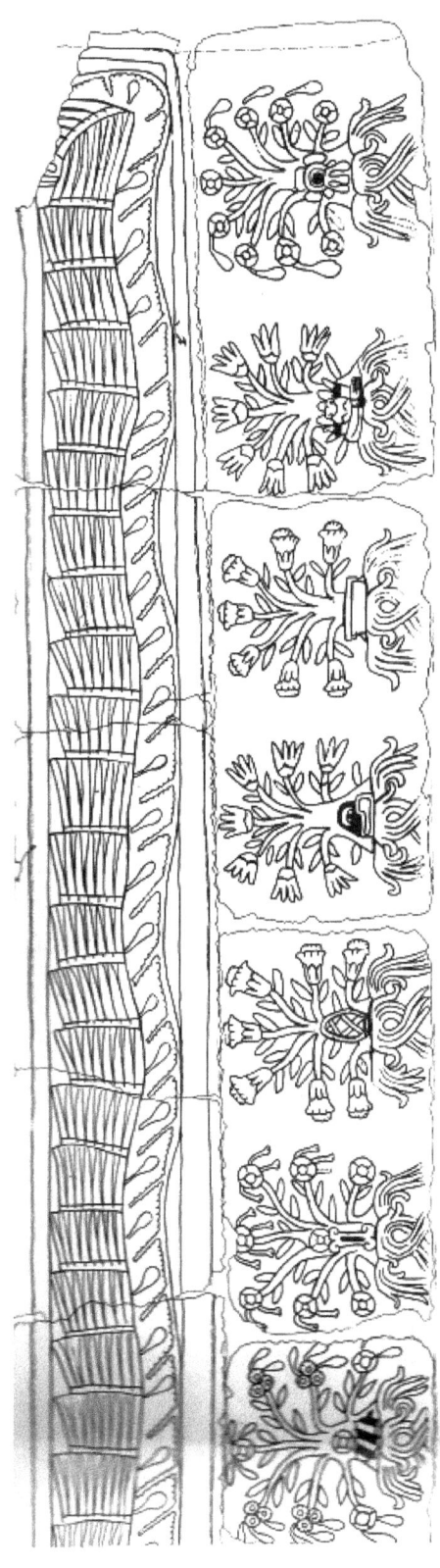

Figure 10. Wagner Mural Collection; Serpent I. After Berrin *et al.* 1988: Fig.VI.1

Figure 11. Examples of nine different glyph compounds found in the trunks of the flowering trees in the Wagner Mural Collection. (a-i) from Serpent I. After Berrin *et al.* 1988: Fig. VI.1.

Many scholars argue for Teotihuacan writing on the basis of these murals because it is believed by many that the murals contain certain toponyms or place names. These murals are of significant interest because many of them contain signs that are found elsewhere at Teotihuacan. If the Wagner Murals were proven to in fact contain toponyms, there would be promise for further linguistics investigation on them. However, that in and of itself does not signify that the murals are true writing. Toponyms are used in a variety of writing systems and are often found in narrative pictography, like in the case of Aztec pictography. However, the presence of toponyms or calendric signs and dates, for that matter, does not mean necessarily indicate that a true writing system is in use. "Although the chief aim of writing is not artistic effect but the practical recording and transmission of communication, writing at all times has had elements of aesthetic value" (Gelb 1952: 229).

The Language of Teotihuacan

The language that the inhabitants of Teotihuacan spoke has always been the subject of debate because little is known about this civilization. Although there have been many hypotheses about the language of Teotihuacan, a logical explanation, adopted by many scholars, seems to come from pure and simple geographical circumstances.

The Nawa language, which comes from the southern branch of the Yuta-Nawan (often referred to as Yuta-Aztecan) stock/family is the most appealing language to non-linguists as the Teotihuacan language. This may be, in part, because many varieties of Nawa were and are still spoken in Central Mexico. Nawa has an internal time depth of 1,500 years, approximately 1,316,000 speakers, and is one of the most numerous linguistic entities in Mesoamerica (Kaufman 1994: 34).

The two other great civilizations that flourished between two and six centuries later in the Basin of Mexico, the Toltecs and the Aztecs, both spoke varieties of Nawa. Therefore it makes sense, on the surface, that the Teotihuacanos spoke Nawa, or a closely related dialect, as well. These civilizations, undoubtedly, contributed largely to the increase of Nawa speakers throughout Mexico. "The Toltec influence was responsible for the spread of Nawa loans into many languages of Mesoamerica (Kaufman 2001b ms)." Linguistic evidence is extremely important to the proper identification of the Teotihuacan language. "Although Nawa has had a persistent appeal to archaeologists as the dominant language of the inhabitants of Teotihuacan, the contrasts between the nature, extent, and era of influence by Mesoamerican languages on Nawa with that of Nawa on other Mesoamerican languages make it exceedingly implausible that Nawas played a leading role at Teotihuacan" (Kaufman 2001b ms).

Although Lyle Campbell (1988) does not rule out Nawa and asserts that there are "some suggestive tidbits that might lead us to suspect that it's been around longer than we think", he favors Totonac as the most likely language for Teotihuacan (Cowgill 1992: 240-243). George Cowgill also has proposed that the dominant language in early Teotihuacan was Totonac (or possibly something else) and that late in the city's history Nawa speakers infiltrated, perhaps rather peaceably, and made their language important within the city some time before its destruction (Cowgill 1992: 242). Soren Wichmann (1995, 1998) also offers evidence that he thinks supports the hypothesis that there were Nawa speakers at Teotihuacan during its heyday. However, Kaufman does not accept that Nawa speakers were influencing other Mesoamericans before about 800 CE, which is after the decline of Teotihuacan (Kaufman 2001b ms). Following Cowgill, Campbell and Wichmann, Chadwick also argues for Totonac or maybe Mije-Sokean.

The Nawa language assumption can be disproved quite straightforwardly. We know that Teotihuacan flourished during the time period of roughly 100 CE–600 CE. Although there is no exact date, it is estimated that the decline of Teotihuacan was somewhere between 500–600 CE. "Since 500 CE is the approximate time of the demise of the Teotihuacan civilization, and the archaeological record shows evidence of new and simpler cultural patterns in the Basin of Mexico about that time, the simplest way of integrating the data on loan-words from Nawa with the lexicostatistic data is to assume that Nawa came into Mesoamerica from the north about 500 CE (Kaufman 2001a ms)." It would have been linguistically impossible for the Teotihuacanos to have spoken a language that was not present in the area until close to or after its decline. Therefore, linguistic data subverts the possibility of the language of Teotihuacan having been Nawa.

Kaufman (2001b ms) examines the results of linguistic diffusion in pre-Columbian Mesoamerica and concludes that the base population of Teotihuacan was Totonac speaking and the elite population spoke a Mije-Sokean language. "A wide familiarity with linguistic borrowing in

Mesoamerica leads to the recognition that even in situations of language contact over several generations, Mesoamerican languages did not borrow much from each other in Pre-Columbian times (Kaufman 2001b ms)."

Kaufman has identified Mije-Sokean loan words in central Mexico associated with Teotihuacan elites from 100–500 CE, Totonac loan words from outside central Mexico associated with Teotihuacan militarism from 100–500 CE, and Totonac loans into Nawa when Nawas invaded the Basin of Mexico around 500 CE (Kaufman 2001b ms). Distinctively, the number of Nawa lexical borrowings from Mije-Sokean is 14, and the number from Totonac is 15, which may reflect the relatively low status Nawas would have had upon entering into Mesoamerica (Kaufman 2001b ms).

Although there was no Mije-Sokean speaking population in central Mexico at the time of the Spanish arrival, there must have been a population of Mije-Sokean speakers in or near the Basin of Mexico before 500 CE because general Nawa, which spread out from the Basin of Mexico starting around 800 CE, already had a sizeable number of Mije-Sokean loan words, and its grammar showed the effects of contact with a Mije-Sokean language (Kaufman 2001b ms). Mije-Sokean was a primary source of loan words in Mesoamerican languages until 1500 CE, and also was a principal influence in the *Mesoamericanization* of the Nawa language group.

Kaufman (2001b ms) asserts that Teotihuacan influence on other parts of Mexico that involved conquest, take-over or occupation, would be reflected through both Mije-Sokean (elite) and Totonac (soldierly) loan-words. Some examples to back up the Mije-Sokean (elite) Totonac (base) language theory are detailed by Kaufman:

> "The biggest difference in the nature of lexical diffusion from Totonako and Mije-Sokean is that, except for the non-local 'cacao', all plant names are borrowed from Totonako, suggesting that the base population was Totonako. Two kin terms ('man's brother-in-law', 'man's elder sister') are from Totonako, suggesting that Nawas had family ties with Totonakos. No kin terms come from Mije-Sokean (The possible Mije-Sokean borrowing 'child' refers to a life stage and not a kin type). In contrast, the only two seriously high status items, 'mat', and 'shape-shifter/person' are from Mije-Sokean" (Kaufman 2001b ms).

Proto-Mije-Sokean and Proto-Sokean have been reconstructed by both Kaufman (1963 ms) and Wichmann (1995). With these reconstructions, it would be possible to carry out a detailed study into the possibility of a writing system at Teotihuacan if a larger body of data at the site presents itself in the future.

Decipherment

Although the present work is not a decipherment, I feel it necessary to include a section that deals with the process of decipherment. I do propose that there is substantial evidence for writing at Teotihuacan and therefore the possibility for a complete decipherment in the future, if more data emerges at the site.

When dealing with a set of signs that may be part of a writing system, the only true way to determine their meanings is through decipherment. Decipherment is the determining of the values of signs and reading texts represented by signs in particular, no-longer spoken, languages. In most cases, these languages, mostly ancient, have to be reconstructed from proto and/or mother languages before a decipherment can be carried out. The techniques of decipherment are various and not every decipherment requires the use of all techniques (Kaufman and Justeson 2001 ms).

Before attempting any type of decipherment, one must a) have a hypothesis as to which language is represented in the data and b) the capacity to recognize all of the grammatical properties of the language that is hypothesized as being represented in the data. In addition, when looking at the decipherment of a writing system, one must take into careful consideration the possible type of writing system that could have been in use.

Decipherment is a process of accounting for the patterns of sign use in texts (Justeson and Kaufman 1993: 1703) and is certainly not a rushed process. There are many steps that need to be taken to ensure that every aspect is accounted for. The main steps include text preparation, linguistic preparation and an understanding of cultural references. By cultural references, it is meant that one should have a great deal of insight as to specific traits of the studied culture. In this case, a vast knowledge of culturally what encompasses Mesoamerica. Many representations found in Mesoamerican iconography and writing systems are culture-specific to Mesoamerica, and are readily identifiable if you have the proper ethno-historical background.

Text preparation includes 1) documentation of the texts, 2) analysis of texts and establishing coordinates for each text, 3) dating of the text must be achieved or attempted, 4) a sign catalog of the all the signs must be made, 5) a concordance showing the context of every instance of every sign must be created, 6) sign distributions and recurrent combinations of signs must be cataloged, 7) all calendric and numerical notations must be studied separately and marked off in the text (Kaufman and Justeson 2001: 5-6 ms).

Since the correct identification of the language being represented is necessary before attempting a decipherment, the well-formed hypotheses by Kaufman regarding the languages spoken at Teotihuacan would make it possible to decipher the signs if a) they are in fact a writing system, and b) if in the future there were a large enough sampling of data available to analyze.

Methodology

Although the primary focus of this study was to catalog select signs and glyphic elements found at Teotihuacan, I also conducted basic linguistic tests to establish if the use of signs at Teotihuacan did fulfill some of the characteristics for Mesoamerican writing. Therefore, I compared the glyphs found at Teotihuacan to those of other Mesoamerican writing systems and narrative pictography such as Zapotec, Xochicalco and Aztec. I referenced the work by John Justeson and Terrence Kaufman (1993) on Epi-Olmec writing and also their 1998 manuscript on Xochicalco writing. Xochicalco is of particular interest to this study as it basically rose out of the decline of Teotihuacan, and there are many similarities between the signs found at Teotihuacan and those found at Xochicalco.

The data in this study came from two sources of glyphs and glyph compounds at Teotihuacan. I chose these two specific sources because they were: a) the largest sets of co-occurring glyphs, and b) contain the largest number of glyphs. The first set is found at *La Plaza de los Glifos* (The Glyph Plaza), *La Ventilla* (LV). These glyphs were discovered by Rubén Cabrera Castro (1996a, b) during an excavation carried out between 1992 and 1994. According to Castro, the Plaza dates to Late Tlamimilopa or early Xolalpan (Fig. 4), approximately 300–400 CE (Castro 1996b: 39). In the Plaza, there are 42 distinct glyph groups and potential text layouts. Each is made up of glyphs and glyph compounds found at LV. Aside from a few examples on adjoining walls, the red-painted glyphs occur on the central patio floor, with each text in a quadrangle delineated by red lines (Taube 2000: 13). Scholars such as Castro (1996a, b), Langley (1993) and Taube (2000) have all examined the glyphs found at La Ventilla. Although I do not explore it in my work, the fact that the glyphs at La Ventilla are painted red and that they are separated by red lines is noteworthy. Gelb believes that:

> "Meaning can sometimes be conveyed within writing not only by conventional forms of signs but also by various auxiliary methods based on the color. In older times, when all writing was done by hand, color differentiation was found more frequently. Both the old Mexican writings and the more modern writings of the American Indians frequently employ a method of coloring the signs" (Gelb 1952: 18-19).

The second source of glyphs used in my study were from a Mural Painting (MP) found in a structure adjoining the Pyramid of the Sun. Specifically, the mural was located in Zone 5A, room 23 at the site (de la Fuente 1995). The MP is no longer at the archaeological site and is now located in the INAH (Instituto Nacional de Antropología e Historia) conservation laboratory. The MP contains well over two hundred signs that vary in size and complexity. Langley notes that the MP has not previously been studied in detail, but believes that its symbolism is related to that of the ritual censer (Langley 1993: 136).

Although not cataloged, I examined other mural paintings and ceramics from Teotihuacan for similarities to the glyphs that I cataloged. Glyph frequency is an important factor in the determination of glyph function. If future data emerge, this would permit a more detailed analysis or interpretation of specific glyphs. I also compared the glyphs cataloged from LV and MP to those found elsewhere in Mesoamerica. The purpose of creating the Sign Catalog was to systematically organize the data from LV and MP and present the glyphs, along with a code name for each (some of which have already been devised by other scholars, and some of which I have named) and its frequency. The code name is a label or tag and is not an interpretation of the meaning of a glyph.

Once cataloged properly, the glyphs were studied as to their frequencies, recurrent combinations, and distribution. The frequency of the glyphs, for this study, can be defined as the number of times they occur in the data, thus, glyphs that occur over and over again in the data could be said to have a high frequency. The frequency of glyphs would be important to the determination of their specific function in a writing system. I compared the frequency of readable glyphs that occurred on their own versus readable glyphs that appeared to not stand on their own. When I found a particular glyph of high frequency in the data and categorized it as a "readable glyph that could not stand on its own", it was noted that glyph could be a possible syllabic sign, and therefore also indicate inflection on a verb. Recurrent combinations of glyphs would be defined as glyphs that recurrently show up by each other or as part of a glyph compound in the data.

A glyph compound is one or more glyphs put together (Fig. 12). Glyph compounds are found in all Mesoamerican writing systems and generally serve to represent words, which cannot be represented by a single glyph. Glyph compounds can be verbs with syllabic signs, (Fig. 13), but this isn't always the case. They also spell out personal names and titles (Fig. 14), and often times, instead of creating a new logogram, a writing system will use two existing glyphs to represent a single meaning. Glyph compounding is also found in Mesoamerican iconography that is not writing, such as in Aztec toponyms (Fig. 15). The distribution of glyphs is important because if certain glyphs only occur in certain zones at the site, this could be a clue as to their function. For this reason, I evaluated exactly where the LV and MP glyphs occurred in the data, and if they co-occurred in the same zones. In an attempt to establish glyph function, I compared the distribution of the glyphs to that of the syntactic categories of the Proto-Mije-Sokean language.

Figure 12. Example of a glyph compound from La Ventilla, Teotihuacan. After Cabrera Castro, 1996b:33.

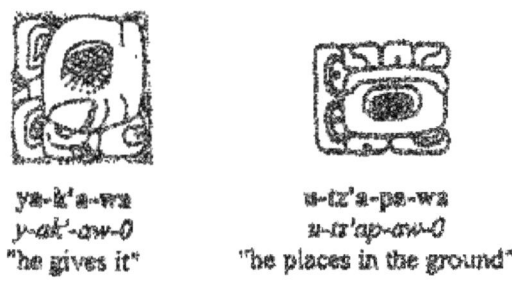

Figure 13. Glyph compounds of verbs with syllabic signs. After Schele and Grube 2002: p. 28.

Figure 14. Glyph compound of a Maya Personal Name. After Harris and Stearns 1997: fig. 5.5.

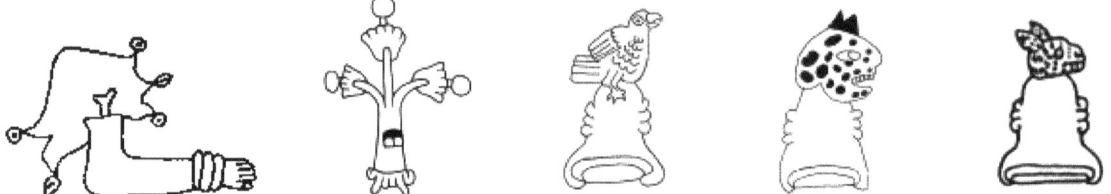

Figure 15. Examples of different glyph compounds that are Aztec toponyms (place names), from the Codex Mendoza.

      For the process of identification (specific to Mesoamerican writing), I conducted tests in the following order: 1) Identify any and all of the calendric elements in the data; 2) Determine when calendric elements are referent of dates or of personal names (Fig. 16); 3) Identify probable personal names (in the form of a glyph compound) and year bearer glyphs (which are part of the Mesoamerican calendar) (Fig. 17); 4) Identify which glyphs might encode nouns (Fig. 18), and which signs might encode verbs (Fig. 13); 5) Parse the texts and look for verbal and/or non-verbal clauses; 6) Examine the chronology and accuracy of the events; 7) Examine the ordering of the glyphs with respect to the syntax of Proto-Mije- Sokean Language.

Figure 16. Calendric element referent of a personal name; "Overlord 7 Rabbit'; Xochicalco, Morelos. After Kaufman and Justeson 1998.

Figure 17. Mesoamerican Year-Bearer glyph from Xochicalco, Morelos. After Kaufman and Justeson 1998.

tu-pa-ja
tu-pa-ja
"earspool"

Figure 18. Mayan glyph that encodes a noun. After Schele and Grube 2002: 34.

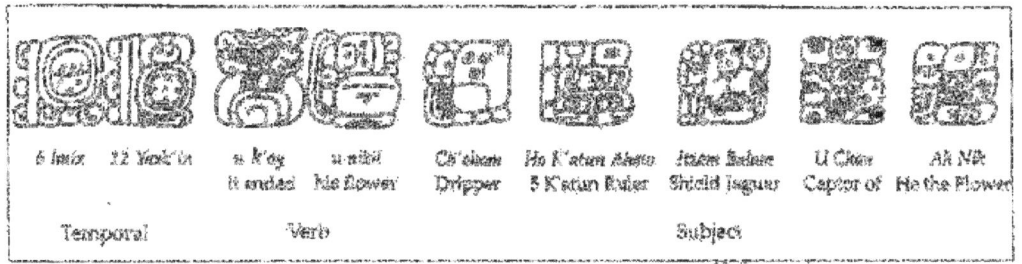

Figure 19. Mayan writing. Clause from the text on Yaxchilan Stela 12. After Harris and Stearns 1997: fig. 5.3.

With the data organized and cataloged in detail, it was possible to begin an analysis that specifically determined if the data fulfilled the requirements of one of the different types of writing systems. I examined the glyph compounds and strings of glyphs with reference to the Proto-Mije-Sokean language. Proto-Mije-Sokean word order is thoroughly left branching; so, glyph compounds and strings of glyphs were examined for syntactic patterns such as adjective noun, genitive noun, post-positions, and relative clause before the noun modifier.

My goal was to look to see if glyphs or similar glyphs from the Teotihuacan data are found in other systems such as Zapotec, Xochicalco and Aztec. After this comparative analysis, the data was examined with reference to logographic systems, then logo-syllabic and phonetic. If it is determined that the data exhibit traits of the criteria required to match the structural pattern of one or more of these systems, it can be concluded that the glyphs probably form a writing system. These criteria will include:

◆ verbal sentences/clauses found in the data;

◆ strings exhibiting left branching word order;

◆ any frequently occurring glyphs that might function as syllabic signs in the data.

The word order of Proto-Mije-Sokean is left branching, therefore any possible verbal sentences/clauses will be laid out in this order. I looked for both verbal and nonverbal sentences/clauses. They are defined as follows after Justeson and Kaufman (1993):

Verbal sentence/clause: *A does something or A does something to B. [SV, SOV]*

Nonverbal sentence/clause: *A is B. [SP ~ PS]*

Since a glyph compound may represent a verb with some of its affixes, the verb in the compound will a) depict an event and b) have affixes. The affixes that will accompany the verb will appear as syllabic signs (Fig. 8), and these signs will occur at a high frequency in the text. To examine the glyphs in search of the verb, I examined glyph compounds and strings of glyphs to look for glyph groups with several components. I then set up two grammatical models to test my data.

These models were the following:

Model 1: Logo-syllabic

- contains a logogram and a phonetic element

Model 2: Logographic

- contains no syllabic signs
- conveys only word order

If after thorough examination of the data, no similarities are found between the iconography and the requirements for these types of writing systems, it can be concluded that the glyphic elements are not that of a writing system, but rather that of complex visual art or narrative pictography.

This outcome would not depreciate the value of my research, as it would help other scholars in the future who may plan to work on this same system. If it is writing, it will reflect some structural feature of the language it represents even if it is only the word order. The goal of this study is to yield a closer examination of the glyphic elements of Teotihuacan in order to determine whether further work in the way of a complete decipherment is a possibility.

Comparative Analysis

The following figures are comparisons of the glyphs from Teotihuacan LV and MP with those found elsewhere at Teotihuacan and in other parts of Mesoamerica. All references and duplications of the glyphs from LV used are from Ruben Cabrera Castro (1996b). All references and reproductions of the glyphs from MP are from a drawing based on slides taken by Rene Millon in 1965.

The LV glyph shown in Figure 20a and Figure 21c below in part, and as a whole resemble glyphs found elsewhere in Mesoamerica and at Teotihuacan called "TWISTED ROOT" and "BUNDLE". This particular glyph from LV has only one occurrence. For this reason, it is difficult to identify it as either. In the sign catalog, a more detailed explanation of the LV glyph is provided. It is possible that this glyph stands alone, or it may form part of a glyph compound.

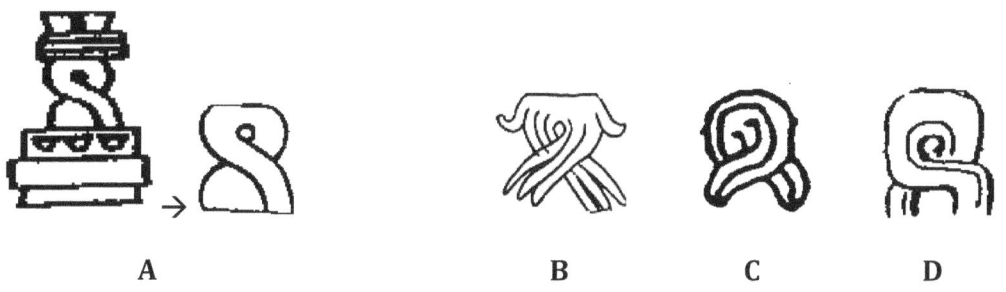

Figure 20. "TWISTED ROOT" glyph variants in Mesoamerica. (a) LV glyph showing detail after Cabrera Castro, 1996b, (b) Teotihuacan Wagner Murals Fragment from Serpent I after Berrin et al. 1988: Fig. VI, (c) Monte Alban, Zapotec site, from Lápida de Bazán, after Orcid 2001: Fig. 5.61, (d) Temple of the Plumed Serpents, Xochicalco after Seler, 1904.

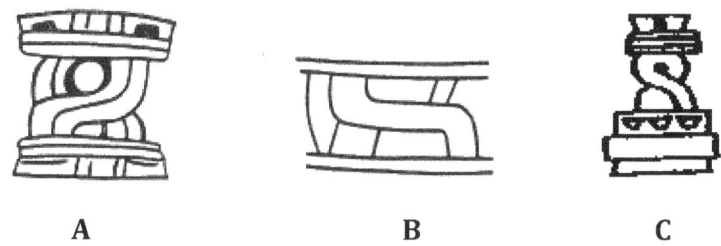

Figure 21. Possible "BUNDLE" variants at Teotihuacan. Several scholars such as Seler and von Winning have identified glyphs similar to "TWISTED ROOT" as "BUNDLE". (a) and (b) from Langley 1986: Fig. 32, (c) LV after Cabrera Castro, 1996b.

Figure 22. Teotihuacan style glyphs found at the Zapotec site of Monte Alban from the *Lápida de Bazán*. The carved stone slab illustrates the glyphs from Monte Alban. The figures below it show the Teotihuacan glyphs (left) alongside similar glyphs from the slab (right). LV Glyphs after Cabrera Castro, 1996b.

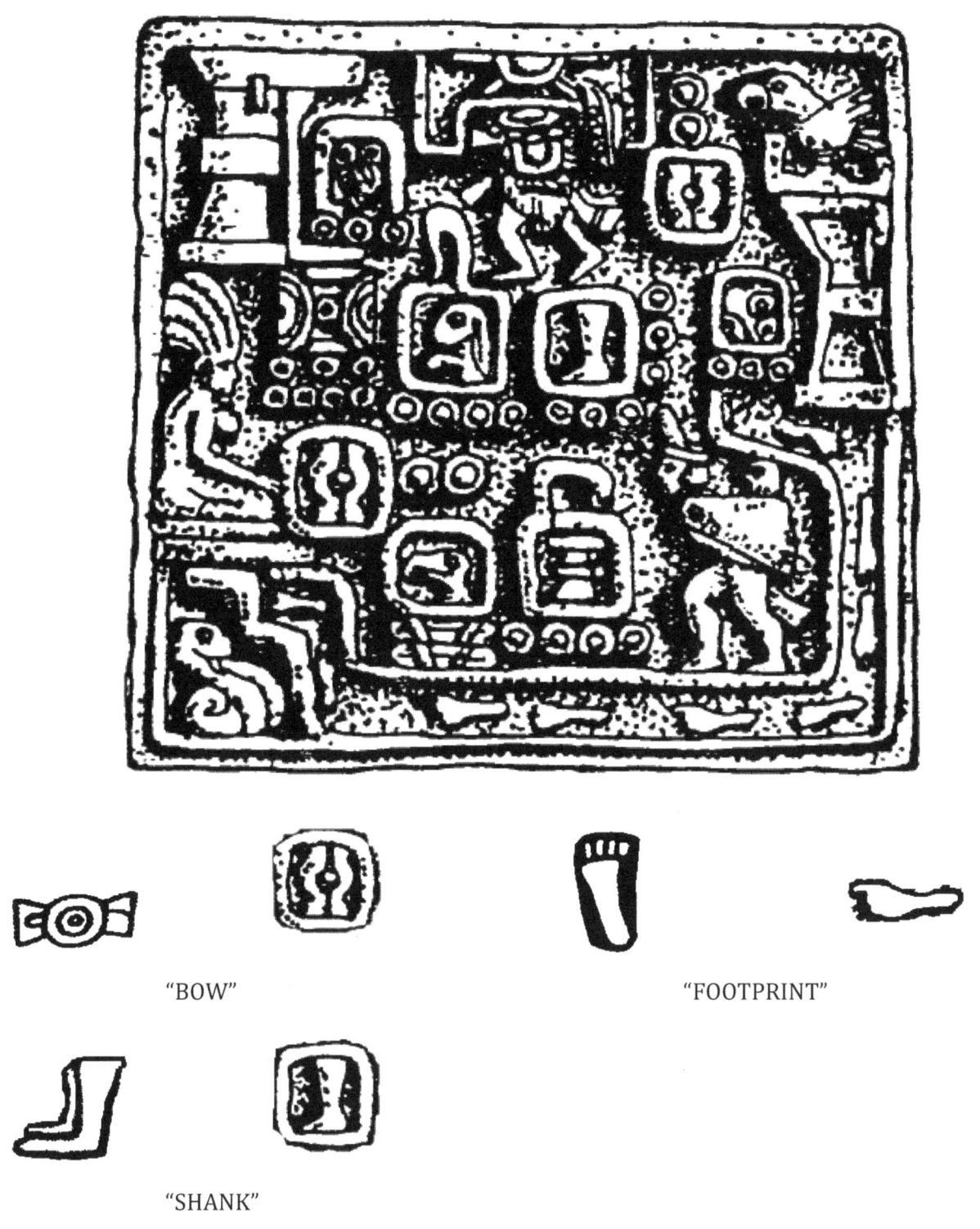

Figure 23. Teotihuacan style glyphs found at Xochicalco, Central Mexico. The carved stone slab illustrates the glyphs from Xochicalco. The figures below it show the Teotihuacan glyphs (left) alongside similar glyphs from the slab (right). LV glyphs after Cabrera Castro, 1996b.

"TWISTED ROOT"　　　　"ARROW BUTT"　　　　"MONKEY"

Figure 24. LV glyphs (left) with similar style glyphs from Xochicalco (right). The Xochicalco glyphs similar to "arrow butt" and "monkey" from LV function as day-names in the Mesoamerican calendar. The Xochicalco glyphs are from the Temple of the Plumed Serpents. Xochicalco glyphs after Seler, 1904. LV glyphs after Cabrera Castro, 1996b.

Piedra Labrada　　　　**Teotihuacan**

The stela called *Piedra Labrada* from Vera Cruz contains several Teotihuacan style glyphs, including "ARROW BUNDLE", and "REPTILE EYE". Left is the stela, right are similar Teotihuacan glyphs.

Figure 25. Teotihuacan style glyphs in Vera Cruz. Piedra Labrada glyphs after Caso 1967: pp 150, Fig. 13, Teotihuacan glyphs after Cabrera Castro 1996b, and Millon 1965.

Figure 26. Stela triad, Xochicalco

Similar Teotihuacan Glyphs:

"QUINCROSS" "INTERLOCKED-BANDS" "BOW" "ARROW BUTT"

"FOOTPRINT" "OLD MAN" "MONKEY"

Figure 27. Xochicalco Stelae triad after Saenz 1961, pls. 2-4. Teotihuacan style glyphs found at Xochicalco. LV glyphs after Cabrera Castro, 1996b.

A
Olmec relief
La Venta, Mexico

B
Olmec Monument 13
Southern coast, Guatemala

Teotihuacan glyphs:

"TREFOIL" "BEAD" "FOOTPRINT"

Figure 28. Teotihuacan style glyphs found on Olmec monuments and reliefs. A.) Olmec relief from the southern coast of Guatemala After Joralemon 1971:Fig. 4. B.) Monument 13, La Venta, Tabasco Mexico. After Shook and Heizer 1976:Fig. 2.

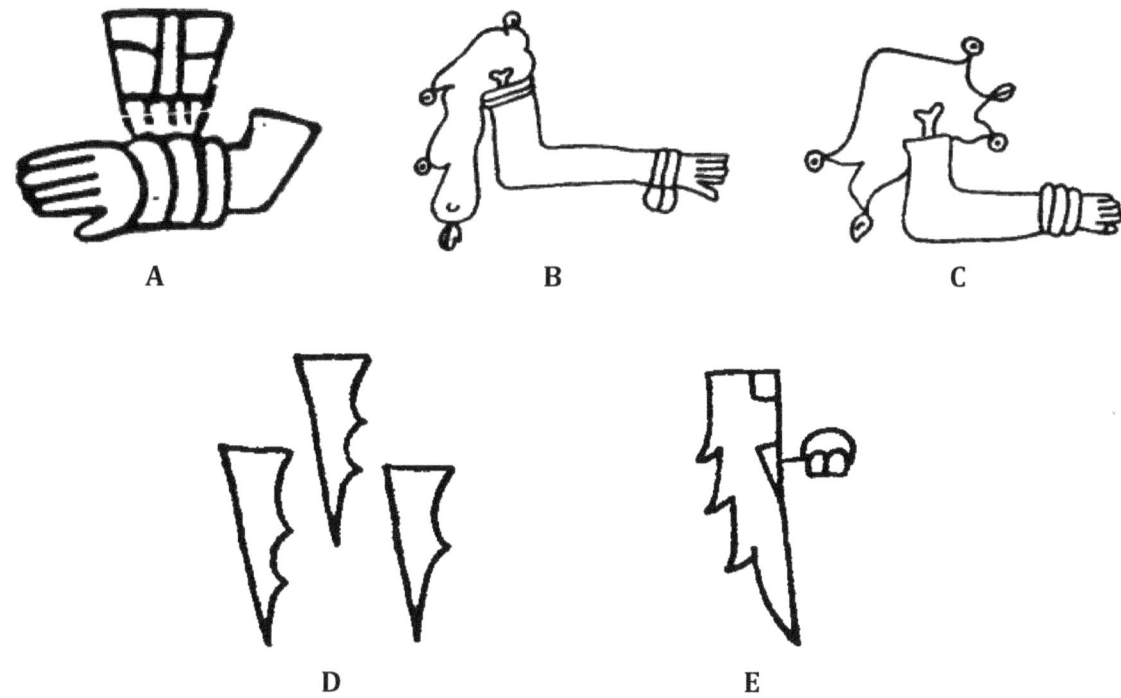

Select Teotihuacan style glyphs found in Aztec Codices.

Figure 29 (a) LV after Cabrera Castro, 1996b; (b) Acolhuacan from the Codex Mendoza; (c) Colima toponym, from Codex Mendoza; (d) Teotihuacan mural fragment; (e) Huitztlan toponym from Codex Mendoza.

The following figures are comparisons of glyphs from Teotihuacan LV and MP with similar glyphs found elsewhere at the site. All references and reproductions of glyphs from MP are from a drawing based on slides taken by Rene Millon in 1965. All references and reproductions of the glyphs from LV are from Ruben Cabrera Castro in 1996b.

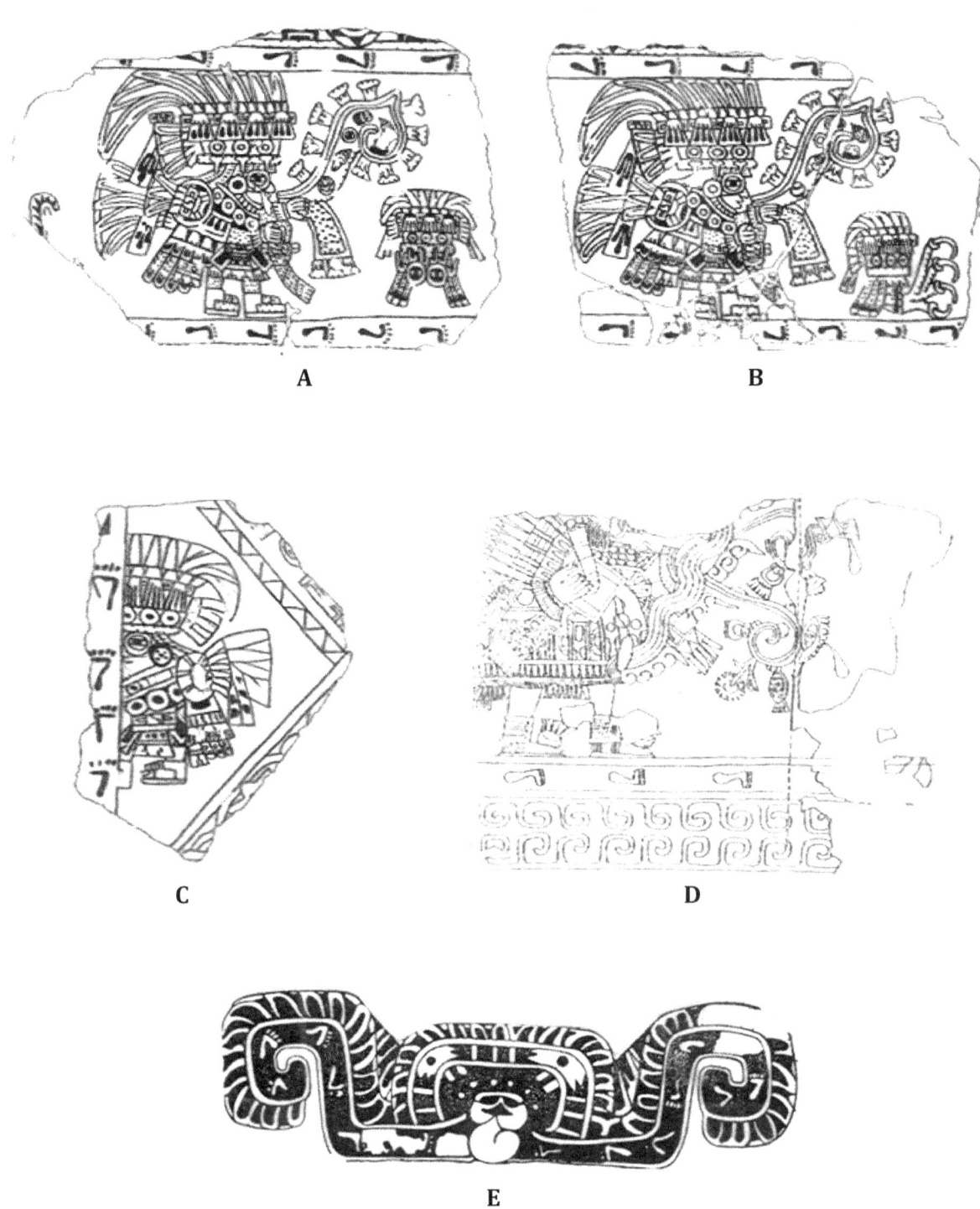

"FOOTPRINT" Glyph

Figure 30. (a); (b); (c); and (d) from Techinantitla apartment compound; (e) from MP. All glyphs from Techinantitla by Saburo Sugiyama 1984.

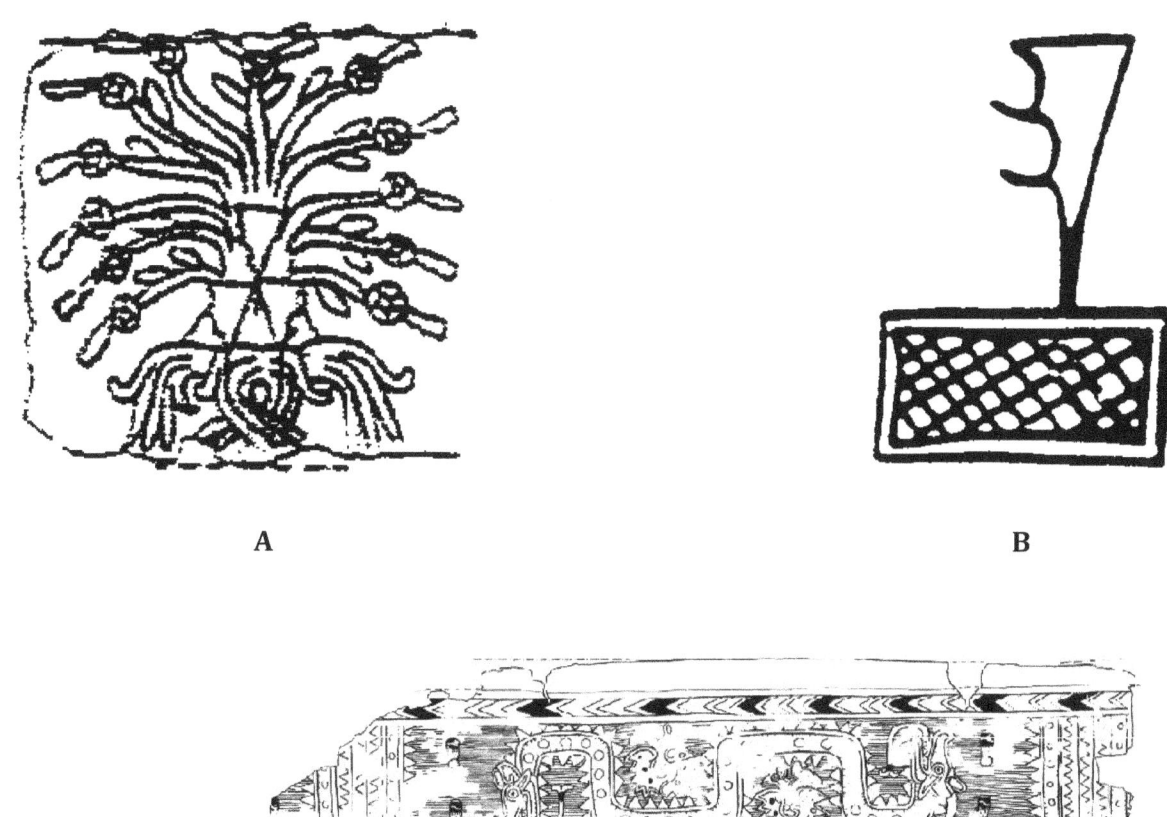

"MAGUEY SPINE" glyph

Figure 31 (a) Tree fragment from the Wagner Mural Collection, Teotihuacan; (b) Maguey spine glyph from LV, (c) Maguey blood-letting ritual mural in a portico, Teotihuacan. Glyphs (a) and (c) by Saburo Sugiyama (1984). (b) by Cabrera Castro, 1996b.

A B

"DEER-SNAKE" glyph

Figure 32 (a) from Coyote and Deer mural painting, Teotihuacan; after Berrin *et al.* 1988: Fig. VII, (b) from La Ventilla, Teotihuacan, after Cabrera Castro, 1996b.

Mural painting found at the Palace of the Sun. Drawing by Felipe Davalos G. in Miller 1973: Fig. 116

Figure 33. Mural painting of Tlalocan, Tepantitla, Teotihuacan with "bug" and "bird" glyphs similar to MP.

Fragment of the Tlalocan mural at Tepantitla, Teotihuacan. After Heyden 1998: pp. 78-79

Figure 34. Mural paintings found near the Palace of the Sun containing various "bug glyphs" similar to those found in MP.

Mural painting found at the Palace of the Sun. Drawing by Felipe Davalos G. in Miller 1973: Fig. 116

Figure 33. Mural painting of Tlalocan, Tepantitla, Teotihuacan with "bug" and "bird" glyphs similar to MP.

Fragment of the Tlalocan mural at Tepantitla, Teotihuacan. After Heyden 1998: pp. 78-79

Figure 34. Mural paintings found near the Palace of the Sun containing various "bug glyphs" similar to those found in MP.

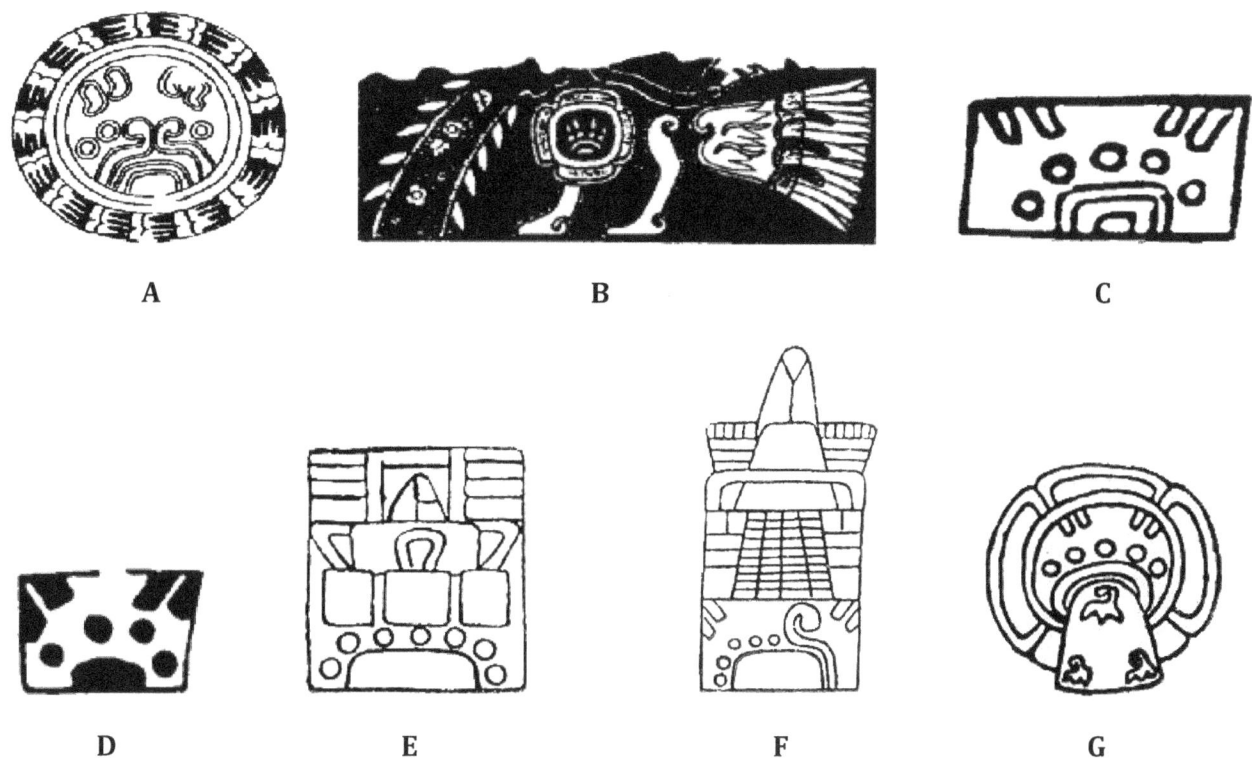

"REPTILE EYE" glyphs.

Figure 35 (a) from Tepantitla, after Miller 1973, Figs. 185 and 187; (b) from Palace of Zacuala, after Séjourné 1959, Fig. 7; (c) LV after Cabrera Castro 1996b, (d) from MP, (e-g) after Caso 1967. Fig 14.

"QUINCROSS" glyph.

Figure 36 (a) from Tepantitla after Séjourné 1956, Fig. 14; (b) LV after Cabrera Castro, 1996b.

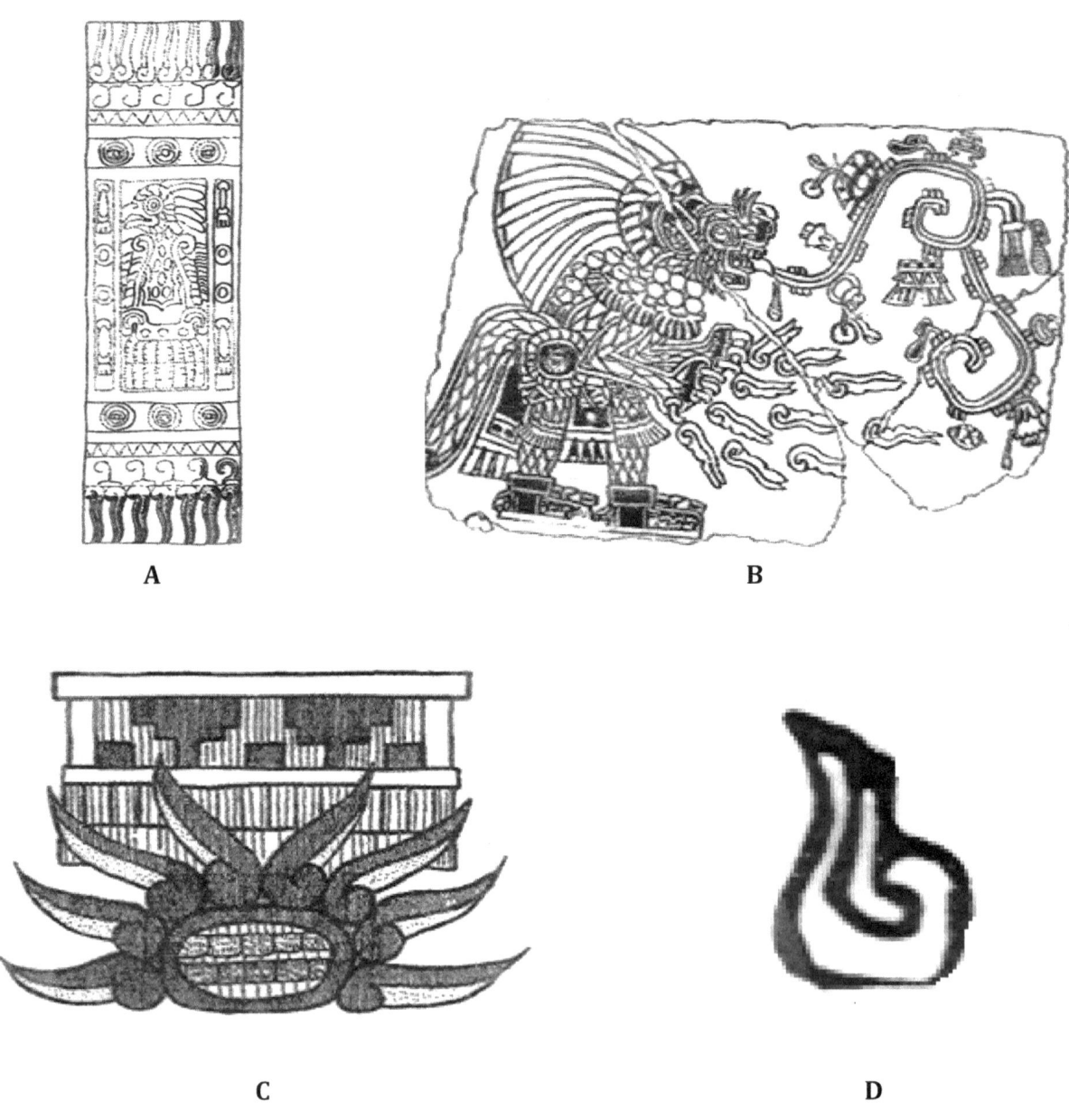

"FLAME" glyph.

Figure 37 (a) from Palace of Quetzalpapalotl, after Acosta 1964: Fig. 103; (b) from Techinantitla, after Berrin *et al.* 1988: Fig. VI. 15; (c) from Tetitla, after Séjourné 1966: Fig. 141 and (d) LV after Cabrera Castro 1996b.

          A   B

"MOUNTAIN" variant glyphs.

Figure 38 (a) from pottery found at Teotihuacan after von Winning 1949:Fig. 3 (b) drawing of tripod vessel containing mountain variant, and "Reptile Eye" glyphs, after Kubler 1967:Fig. 30.

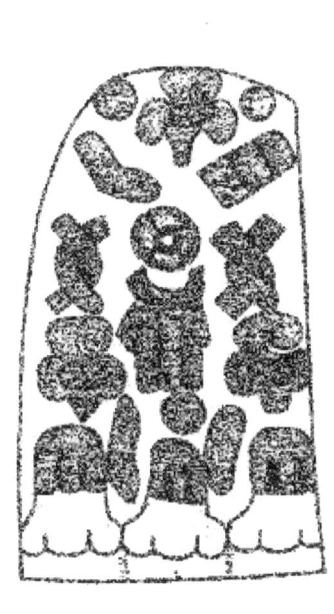 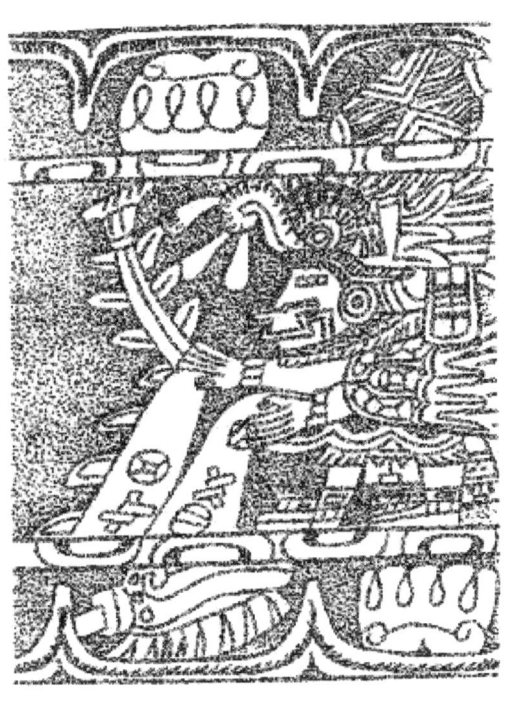 

      A   B   C

"GLYPH CLUSTERS"

Figure 39 (a) Core Cluster with "BELL FLOWER", TREFOIL", "INTERLOCKED BANDS", "BENT BAR", "DOT", "FRONT FACING FLOWER" and "NOSE PLUG" glyphs similar to MP. The Cluster was reconstructed from two fragmentary *adornos*. Museo Diego Rivera de Anahuacali, Mexico City. Drawing by James C. Langley in Berrin *et al.* 1993, (b) Relief from Tetitla with "INTERLOCKED BANDS", "FRONT FACING FLOWER" and "BELL FLOWER" glyphs similar to MP. Relief after Séjourné 1966: Fig. 38, and (c) Core Cluster incised on a tablet with "INTERLOCKED BANDS", "NOSE PLUG", "TREFOIL", and "FRONT FACING LOWER" similar to MP, from a private collection, after Langley 1992: Fig. 30.

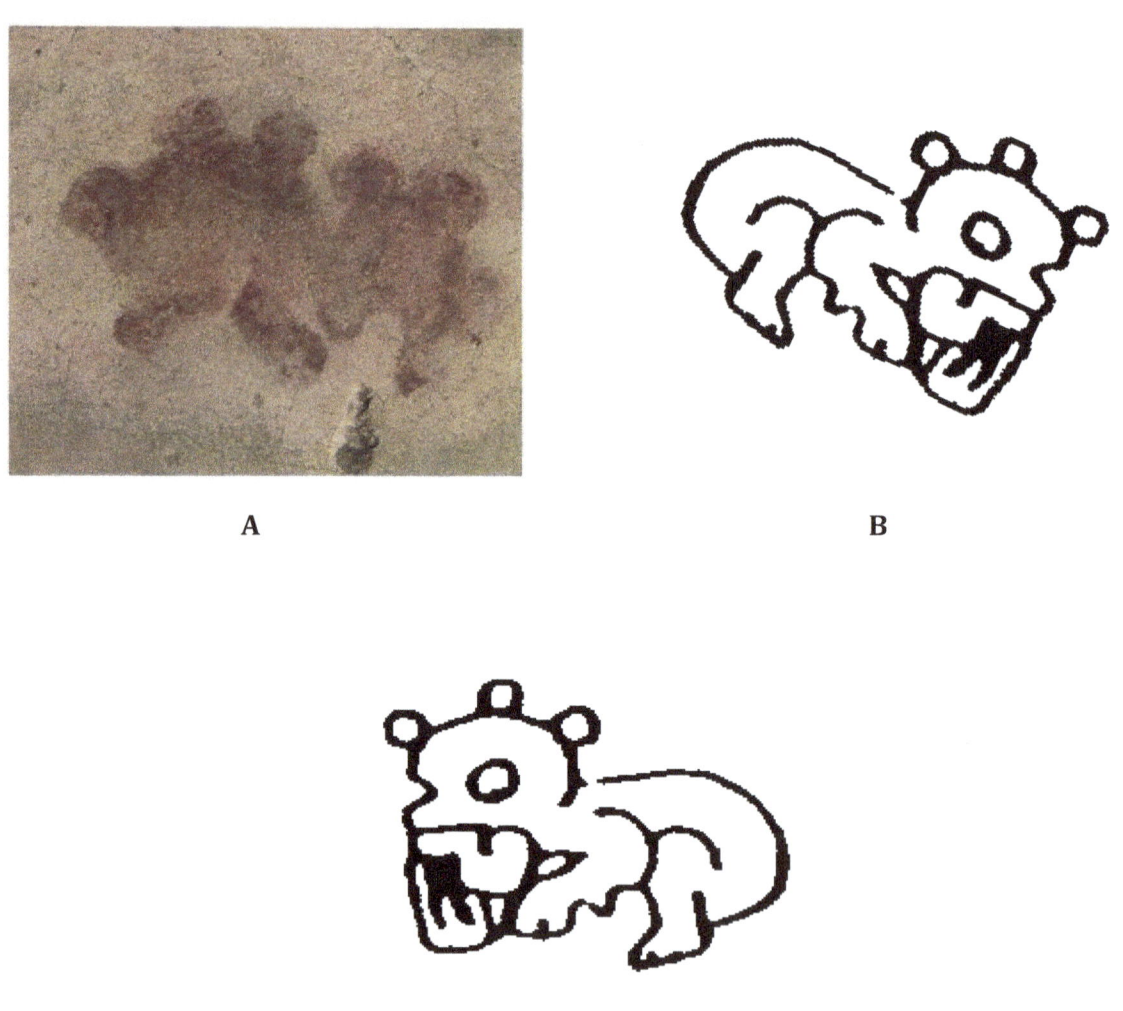

A   B

C

"WATER MONSTER" and Animal Motifs at Teotihuacan

Figure 40. Figure 30 (a) is one of six animals painted on the floor at Tetitla, Portico 24, (b) is the glyph I call "WATER MONSTER" from MP (I have changed the orientation from the original to compare it to that found at Tetitla, (c) is the "WATER MONSTER" glyph from MP in its original orientation in the mural painting. Fig. 30 (a) from Miller 1973.

Although the animal motifs found at Tetitla are not detailed, their outline is almost identical to the glyph from MP, which I call "WATER MONSTER". I believe that this can not be overlooked. The other interesting thing to not with the animal motifs from Tetitla is that they were painted on the floor of the Portico and painted in red, as where the glyphs from LV. Although the animal motifs have no similarities with those of the Plaza floor at LV, it is noteworthy that they were in fact painted on the floor.

Speech and Sound Scrolls

In Mesoamerica, the scroll usually denotes an utterance. If found originating from the mouth of a human figure, they are referred to as "speech scrolls". When they are found originating from the mouth of animal figures or innanimate objects, they are referred to as "sound scrolls". The use of speech and sound scrolls that carry glyphic elements is found throughout Mesoamerica (Fig 41). Many of the speech scrolls associated with individuals in the Tepantitla mural carry glyphic elements (Fig 42). Some of these scrolls have only one glyphic element attached to them, (Fig 42d) while others involve a series of glyphic elements that could to be "texts".

In Teotihuacan, glyphic elements associated with both speech and sound scrolls can be attached to the outside of the scroll, found on the inside of the scroll or both (Fig. 43). These strings of text-like glyphs appear to contain specialized information as they are affixed or infixed to the scroll. Scrolls are associated not only with speech or sound in Mesoamerica, but also with nobility rather than commoners.

In a closer examination of the glyphic elements attached to speech scrolls from Tepantitla, I have found certain glyphs that resemble those from MP and LV. In Figure 42a, three glyphic elements are attached to a series of speech scrolls of an individual. Two of the glyphs can clearly be identified as being part of the MP tradition. Those glyphs are "MOUNTAIN" and "BUTTERFLY". In 42b possibly "POD" or "MIRROR", in Figure 42c, possibly "ECCENTRIC FLINT" and in Figure 42d, the glyph attached to the speech scroll resembles the LV "OLD MAN" glyph.

Not all Tepantitla glyphic elements show similarities with LV and MP ones, but those that do deserve recognition. Any glyphic elements that demonstrate a similar style as those from LV and MP are important to this study, especially with reference to the LV glyphic elements, which are more selective as to their locations.

"SPEECH SCROLLS" which carry glyphic elements in other parts of Mesoamerica.

Figure 41. (a) After Codex Mendoza Fig. 121, pp.185, (Berdan and Anawalt 1997) (b) after Codex Selden, pp. 7, (Caso 1964) (c) after Codex Bodley, pp.9,(Caso 1960) (d) after Florentine Codex: book 8, folio 33v, (Sahagún, 1950-1982) (e) after Tira de Tepechpan 9-10, Fig. 132 (Boone 2000), (f) after Codex Mendoza, Folios 65r and 68r, (Berdan and Anawalt 1997) and (g) after Codex Xolotl, pl. 8. (Dibble 1951, 1980).

Figure 42. Examples of Tepantitla, Teotihuacan speech scrolls, which carry glyphic elements. Figure 31 (a) from Angulo 2001: Fig. 4.28, pp. 152; (b) from Angulo 2001: Fig. 4.29, pp. 153; (c) from Angulo 2001: Fig. 4.31, pp. 154; and (d) from Angulo 2001: Fig. 39, pp. 238.

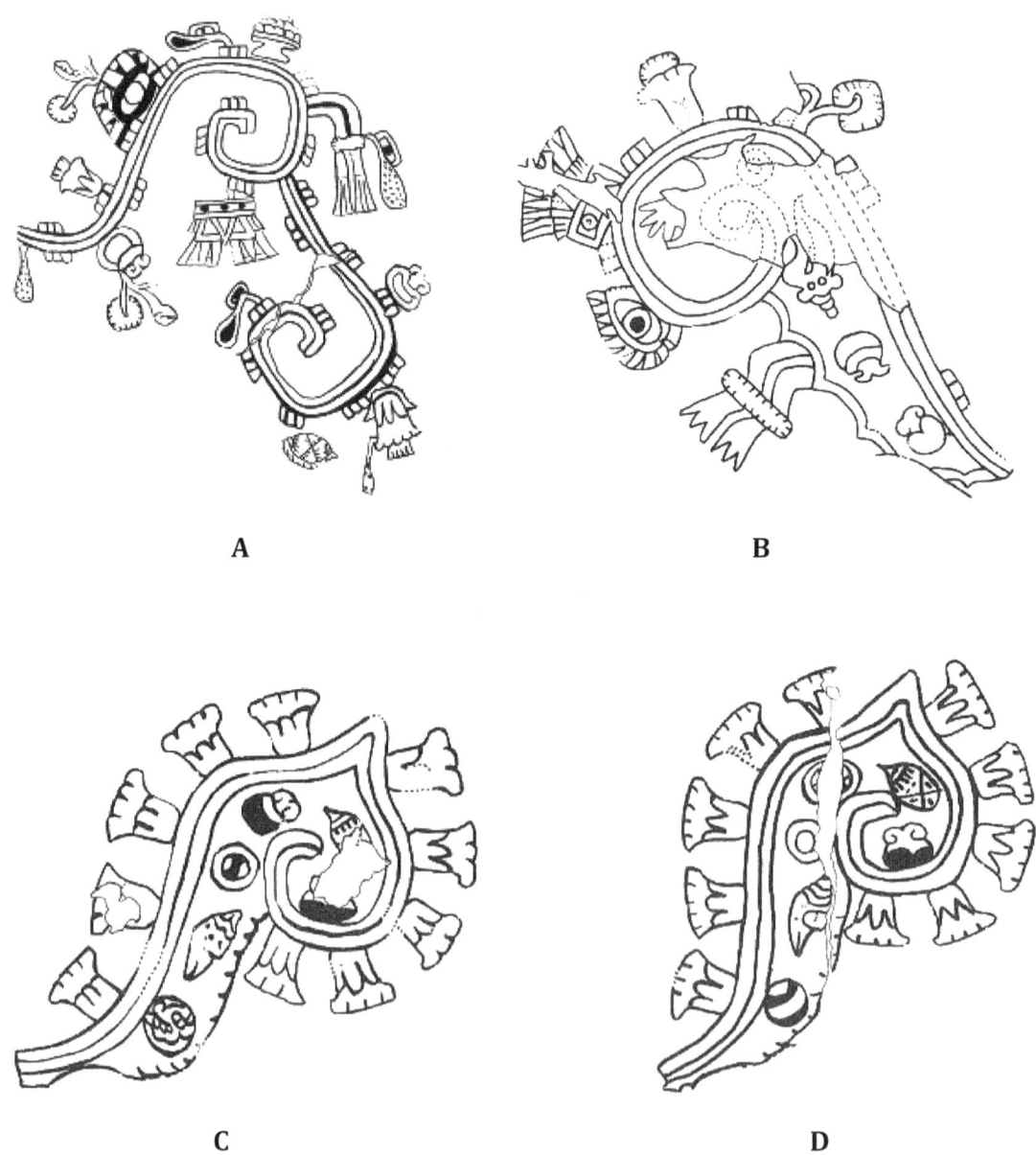

Figure 43. Examples of glyphic elements attached to the outside or found inside of speech scrolls. Figure 33 (a) Feathered Feline Mural, (b) Maguey Bloodletting Ritual Scene Mural, Tlacuilapaxco, (c) Figure with Headdress Scene, Techinantitla, (d) Figure with Headdress Scene, Techinantitla. All found in Berrin *et al.* 1988.

The above examples in Figure 43 illustrate specialized sound and speech scrolls that carry glyphic elements attached to the outside of the scroll, inside of it and both. They have similarities with those found at LV and MP such as "BELL FLOWER", "SCROLL ADORNMENT BAR", "TREFOIL", "SHELL", "CONCH", and "WATER LILLY".

The next pages will present a sign catalog of the glyphic elements at Teotihuacan presented in two sections; one dedicated to the glyphic elements of The Plaza of the Glyphs at *La Ventilla* (LV) and the other from the Mural Painting adjoining the Pyramid of the Sun (MP). This sign catalog is an organized way of presenting the glyphs, but is not an interpretation of the meanings of the glyphs themselves. All representations of glyphs used in the LV catalog are taken from Ruben Cabrera Castro 1996b, and all representations of glyphs used in the MP catalog are from a drawing based on slides taken by Dr. Rene Millon in 1965.

Choosing names for Glyphs

The names chosen for the glyphs in the sign catalog were selected in a specific way. First, if a name was previously devised for a glyph by another scholar and I do not have what I consider to be a better name for it, that name was used. Second, if a glyph had not been previously assigned a name, a serious name was selected for it. By serious, I mean that a name was devised based on my best judgment of what the glyph could possibly represent for this particular ethnic group on the basis of having an ethno-historical background of the area. Third, if a glyph could not easily be identified or associated with any known Mesoamerican symbolic category, a nickname was assigned to the glyph.

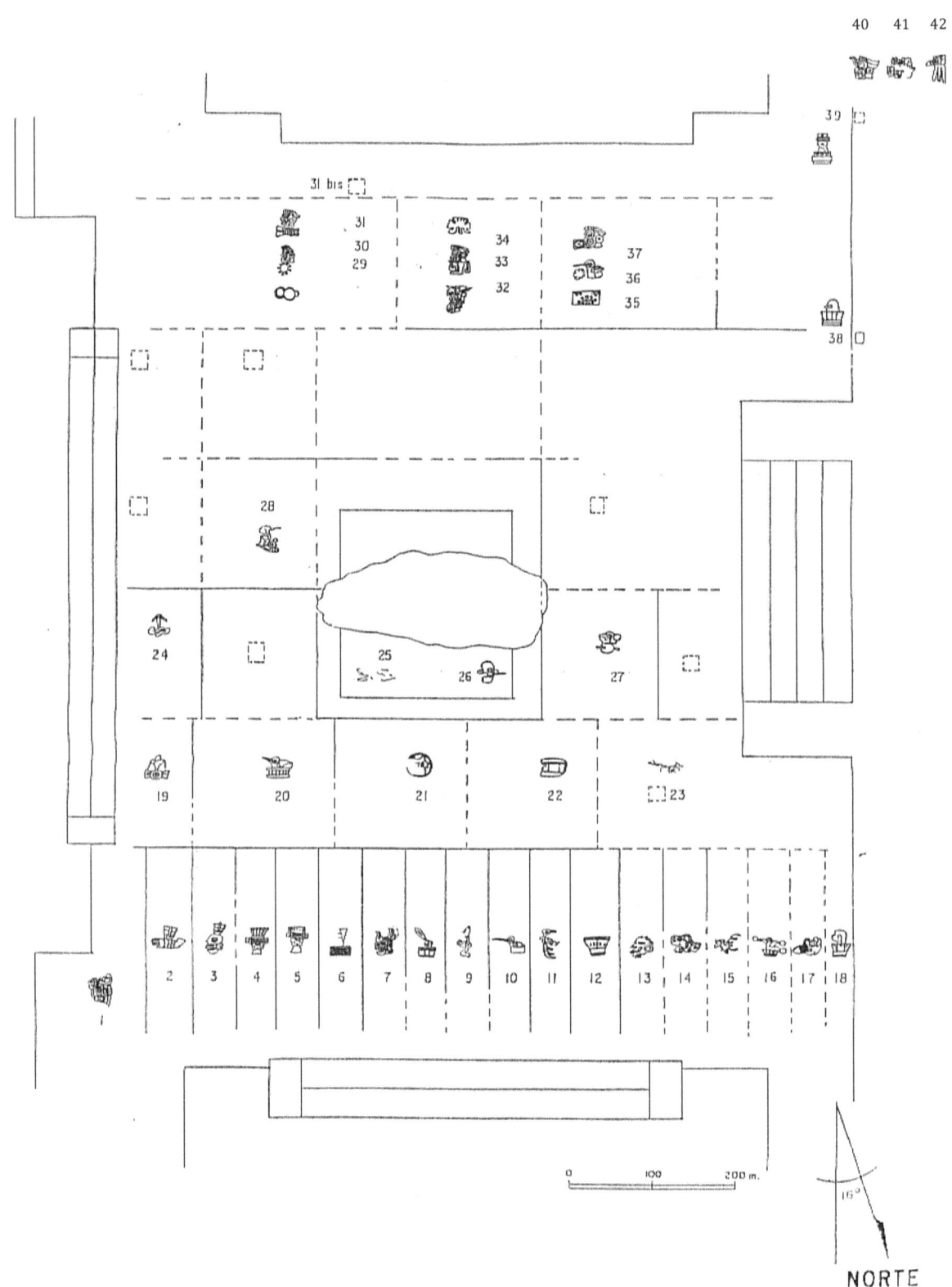

*Plan of the floor of La Ventilla and numbering system 1-39, by Ruben Cabrera Castro, 1996.
*Addition of glyphs, and numbering of glyphs 40, 41 and 42 by the author.
*Glyphs used by the author were taken from Cabrera Castro, 1996b.

The first sets of glyphs presented in this sign catalog are from La Ventilla, Teotihuacan (LV). The LV sign catalog will first present the readable glyphs, followed by unreadable and partially eroded glyphs and lastly readable glyphs that never stand alone.

Readable Glyphs

1. This glyph I call "goggle-eyed-god". It occurs seven times. In all occurrences, the figure faces left. The first occurrence is in position 1. I believe this goggle-eyed figure to possibly represent the pre-Columbian god known in Nawa as *Tlaloc*. It co-occurs with two other glyphs I call "hand" and "eccentric flint". In 32, it appears with another glyph that is positioned above it that I call "headdress". Number 30 occurs with another glyph positioned below it, which Terrence Kaufman has identified as similar to the Epi-Olmec and Zapotec glyphs for the verb "to plant" or noun "seed". It is also found in position 33, and has two different glyphs positioned below it. One I call "shank" and on either side of the "goggle-eyed-god" what James Langley has named "flame". There are two more occurrences in position 31 situated on top of another glyph, which I call "arrow-bundle" and the other in position 37. In 37, it occurs with a glyph affixed to the lower bottom of the face of the google-eyed figure that has been named "quincross" by Langley. The final occurrence is at 40 and has one glyph located in front of it which I call "flame".

2. This glyph I call "netted-jaguar". It appears once in position 14.

14

3. The glyph Karl Taube has named "jaguar-eating-heart" appears two times. In 17, alone, and in 42 with the glyph I call "three feather tassel".

17   42

4. The glyph that Taube has named "jaguar-head and strung-bead" occurs once at 27.

27

* Glyphs 14, 17, 27 and 42 all represent an animal I believe to be a jaguar.

5. The glyph I call "hummingbird" has four occurrences. 10 appears alone, 16 appears with another glyph Kaufman has named "basket", and three other glyphs, which I call "beads". 20 occurs with what I call "drum", and 36 appears with what I call "cotton-ball".

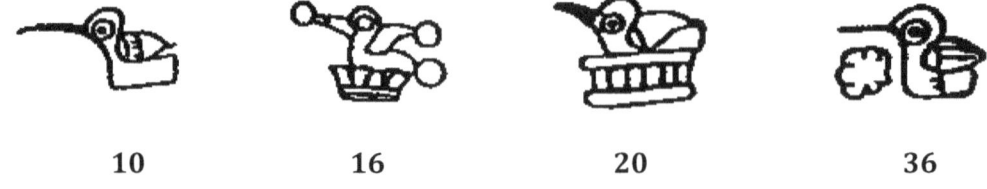

10   16   20   36

6. The glyph I call "skull" has two occurrences. In 3, it occurs with another glyph on top of it which I call "arrow butt". The second occurrence is at 26".

3   26

7. What Taube refers to as the "old man" glyph appears twice. Alone in 13 and in 15 with the glyph I call "speech".

     13   **15**

8. The glyph I call "3 beads" appears once at 29.

29

9. The glyph that Taube refers to in Nawa as *mazacoatl* (deer-snake) appears twice. Once at 9 and once at 11.

    9   **11**

10. The glyph Kaufman has named "threaded bone needle" appears once at 24.

24

11. The glyph I call "maguey spine and cross-hatch" appears once at 6.

6

12. The glyph Rubén Cabrera Castro refers to as "bow" occurs once at 19. It appears with the glyph I call "handle".

19

13. What Hermann Beyer first named the "reptile eye" glyph appears once in position 35.

35

14. What Eduard Seler first identified as the "water lily" glyph appears once in position 34.

34

15. The glyph I call "temple" occurs once at 39. My use of "temple" is to identify this glyph as a single unit, not as a compound. It is unclear if this is a single glyph or a glyph compound. If it were a compound, it could contain as few as three or as many as twelve separate glyphs. I have chosen to treat it as a single glyph, rather than a compound for several reasons. First, no parts of this glyph appear similar to other glyphs found at LV which form glyph compounds, and/or which never stand on their own. Second, because the data available from LV is quite small and there are no other occurrences of this glyph, as a whole or in parts, in the Plaza of the Glyphs. Interestingly, if taken as a compound, one part of this glyph is similar to the proposed "twisted root" glyphs (Fig. 20) seen elsewhere at Teotihuacan and throughout Mesoamerica. If taken as a single unit, however, it resembles several probable "bundle" glyphs (Fig. 21) found elsewhere at Teotihuacan.

39

16. The glyph I call "drum" has three occurrences. At 5, it appears with two glyphs below it, which I call "belt" and "nose-plug". 8 appears with a glyph above it which I call "needle". 20 appears with "hummingbird" and 22 appears alone.

      8   **20**   **22**

17. The glyph Kaufman refers to as "basket" has four occurrences. 12 appears alone, 16 with "hummingbird" and three "bead" glyphs. 18 with "handle" and 38 with "handle".

    12   **16**   **18**   **38**

Unreadable and partially-eroded glyphs

18. Object 21

21

19. Object 23

23

20. Object 25

25

21. Object 28 is a partially-eroded glyph or glyph compound. A part appears to be a representation of the goggle-eyed figure, which occurs in numerous places at LV.

28

22. Object 41 is a partially-eroded glyph or glyph compound. Three glyphs can be identified as "arrow butt", "flame" and "handle". The remainder is unreadable.

41

Readable glyphs that never stand alone

23. "eccentric flint" once at 1.

24. "hand" once at 1.

25. "arrow butt" appears at 2, 3 and 41.

26. "bound arm" once at 2.

27. "belt" appears at 4 and 5.

28. "nose-plug" appears at 4 and 5.

29. "flame" appears at 7, 33, 40 and 41.

30. "monkey" once at 7.

31. "needle" once at 8.

32. "speech" once at 15.

33. "cotton-ball" once at 36.

34. "handle". Appears at 18, 19, 38 and 41.

35. "strung-bead" once at 27.

36. "headdress" once at 32.

37. "shank" once at 33.

38. "quincross" once at 37.

39. "three-feather tassel" once at 42.

40. "seed" once at 30.

41. "beads" once at 16.

42. "feather tuft", once at 4.

43. "box", once at 5.

44. "arrow bundle" once at 31.

Mural Painting adjoining the Pyramid of the Sun based on slides taken by Rene Millon 1965.

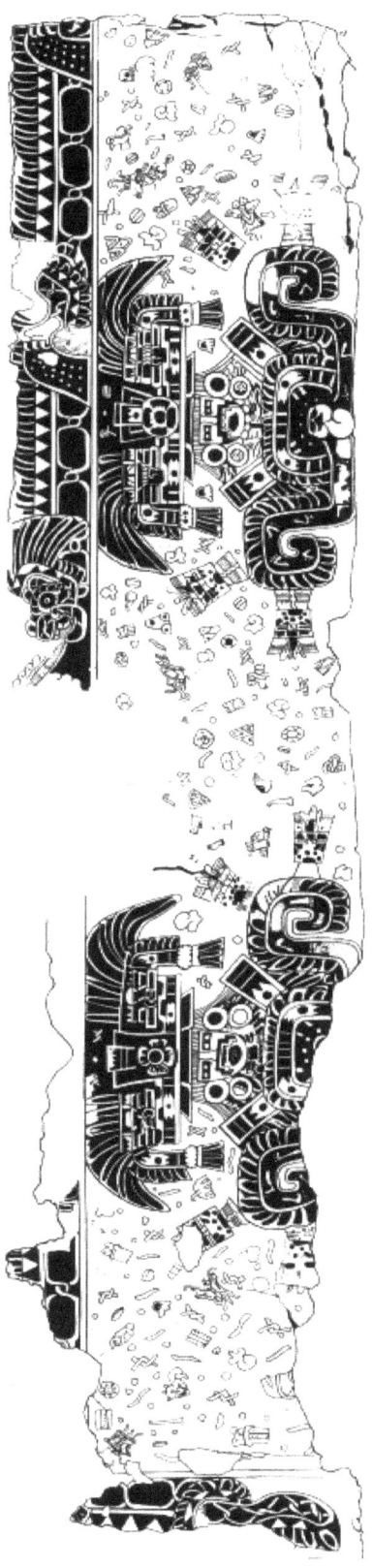

Mural Painting adjoining the Pyramid of the Sun based on slides taken by Rene Millon 1965. Addition of numbering system by the author.

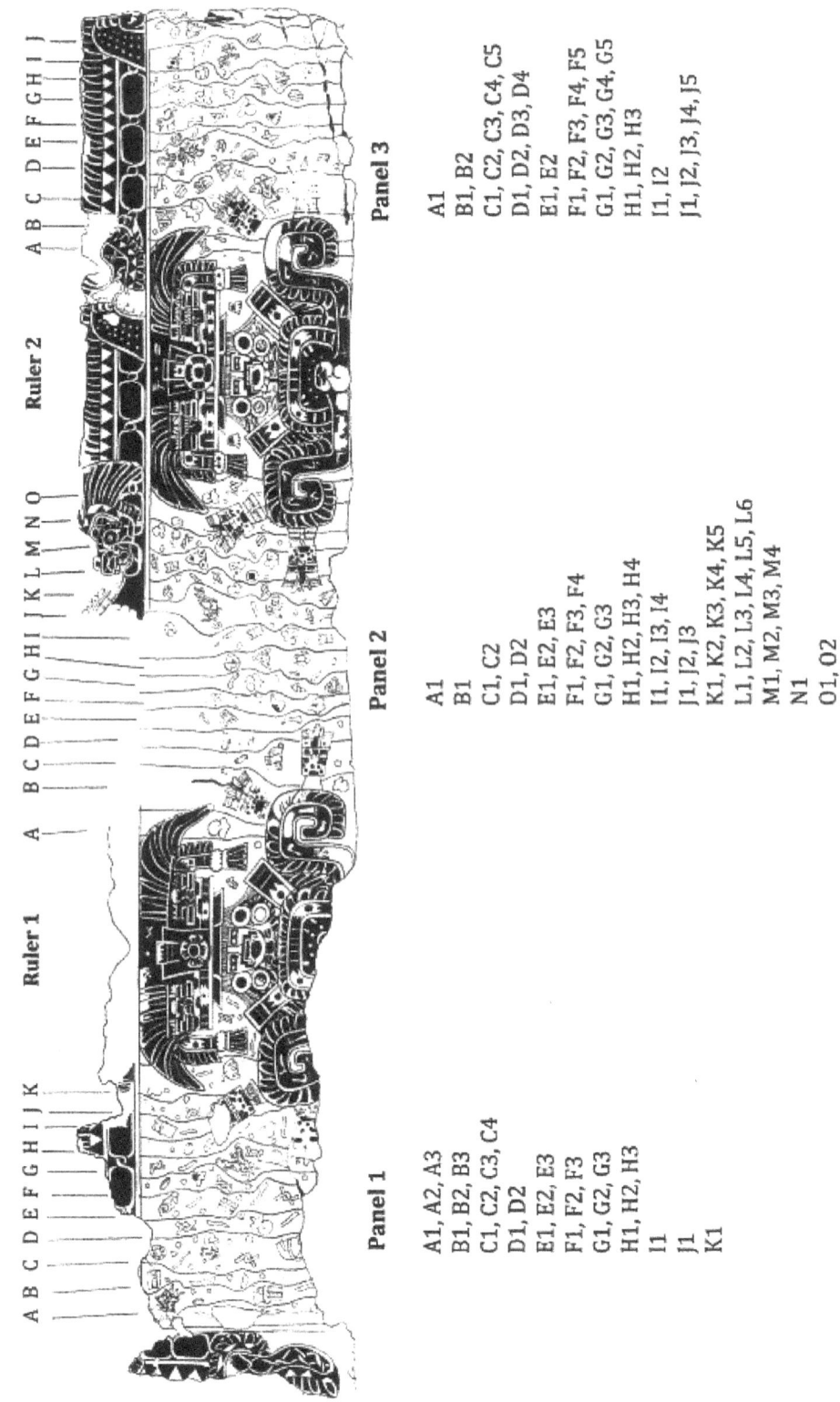

Panel 1

A1, A2, A3
B1, B2, B3
C1, C2, C3, C4
D1, D2
E1, E2, E3
F1, F2, F3
G1, G2, G3
H1, H2, H3
I1
J1
K1

Panel 2

A1
B1
C1, C2
D1, D2
E1, E2, E3
F1, F2, F3, F4
G1, G2, G3
H1, H2, H3, H4
I1, I2, I3, I4
J1, J2, J3
K1, K2, K3, K4, K5
L1, L2, L3, L4, L5, L6
M1, M2, M3, M4
N1
O1, O2

Panel 3

A1
B1, B2
C1, C2, C3, C4, C5
D1, D2, D3, D4
E1, E2
F1, F2, F3, F4, F5
G1, G2, G3, G4, G5
H1, H2, H3
I1, I2
J1, J2, J3, J4, J5

Readable Glyphs

1. The glyph referred to as "butterfly", by scholars such as Langley and Pasztory, is found in Panel 1(P1) P1:A1, P1:F2, P3:I2, and P3:C6. I also use this name for the glyph.

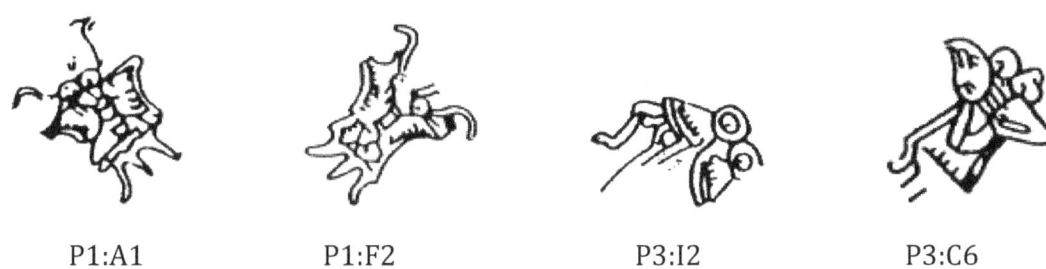

      P1:A1   P1:F2   P3:I2   P3:C6

2. The glyph I call "water monster" occurs at P1:C2.

    P1:C2

3. The glyph Kaufman has named "bird-in-hand" has one occurrence at P1:E1.

    P1:E1

4. The glyph I call "turtle-bird" occurs once at P2:C2.

    P2:C2

5. The glyph I call "grasshopper" occurs once at P2:J1.

P2:J1

6. The glyph I call "bug" appears once at P3:D1.

P3:D1

7. The glyph I call "front-facing flower" is numerous and has several variants.

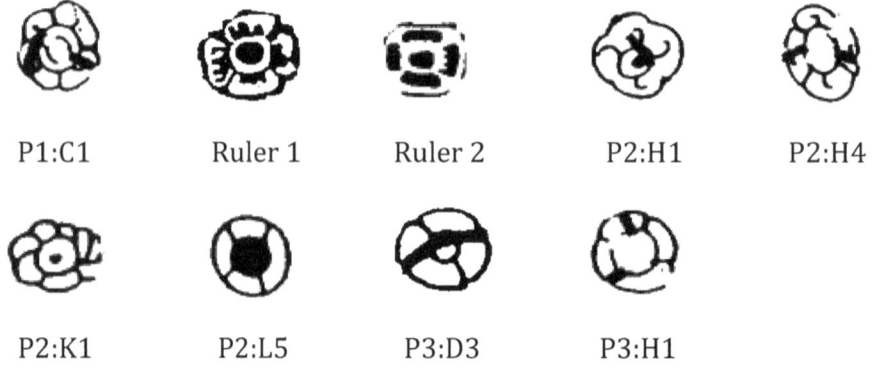

8. The glyph Kaufman named "bell flower" appears several times always with the petals pointing downward. It is found at P1:F2, two times at Ruler #2, and at P3:F5.

9. The glyph I call "interlocked bands" is found at P1:C3, D1, E3, F3, G1, G3, and J1. In Panel 1, all glyphs are in a vertical orientation. In Ruler 1, two times in a vertical and two times in a horizontal orientation. At P2:F1, G2, J3, K2, K4, L1, M3 and O2. In P2:G1 and M3, the glyphs are in a vertical orientation, all others in horizontal. In Ruler 2, the glyph is found once in a vertical orientation. In P3:A1, C1, C5, E2, F3, G1, G2 and J4, all appear in a vertical orientation except for P3:A1, which is horizontal.

Vertical   Horizontal

10. The glyph Kaufman named "leaf" is found at P1:C4 and P1:K1.

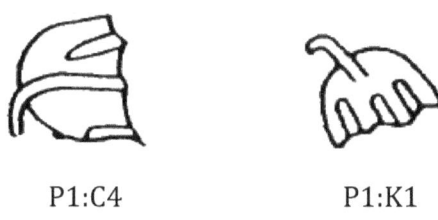

P1:C4   P1:K1

11. The glyph first named "trefoil" by Langley has numerous occurrences. The glyph is found at P1:D2, P2:A1, P2:B1, P2:F4, P2:G1, P2:I3, P2:K3, P2:L6, P2:M1 and P2:O1. It is found once in Ruler 2. In P3:B2, P3:F4 and P3:G2.

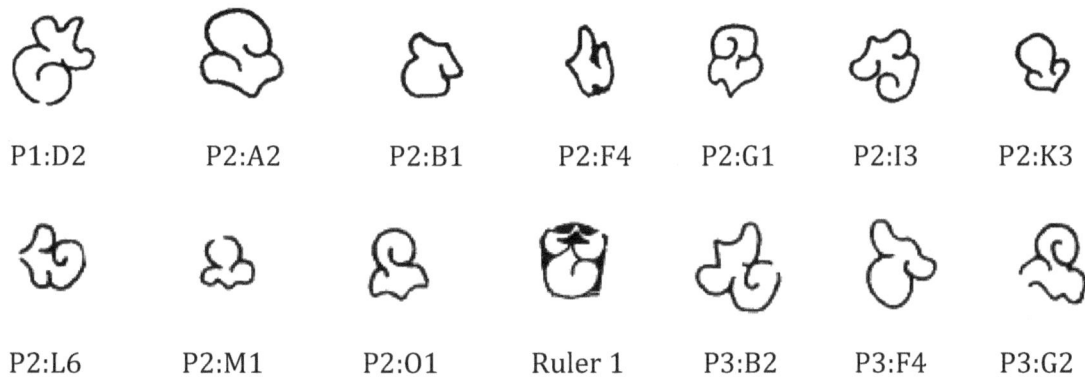

P1:D2   P2:A2   P2:B1   P2:F4   P2:G1   P2:I3   P2:K3

P2:L6   P2:M1   P2:O1   Ruler 1   P3:B2   P3:F4   P3:G2

12. This glyph I call "triple tablet 1" is found at P1:B1.

P1:B1

13. This glyph I call "triple tablet 2" is found at P1:E2.

P1:E2

14. The glyph I call "scroll adornment" is found at P1:H2.

P1:H2

15. The glyph Kaufman named "mirror" is found at P1:H1, P2:M4 and N1, one time at Ruler 2 and P3:C2, E1 and G5.

P1:H2   P2:M4   P2:N1   Ruler 2   P3:C2   P3:E1   P3:G5

16. This glyph I call "pod" is found at P1:A2, P1:F1 and P2:H3.

P1:A2   P1:F1   P2:H3

17. The glyph Langley has named "footprint" only occurs with the two rulers. In Ruler 1, there are seven visible glyphs and they are moving in an outward pattern. In Ruler 2, there are thirteen visible glyphs and they are moving in an inward pattern.

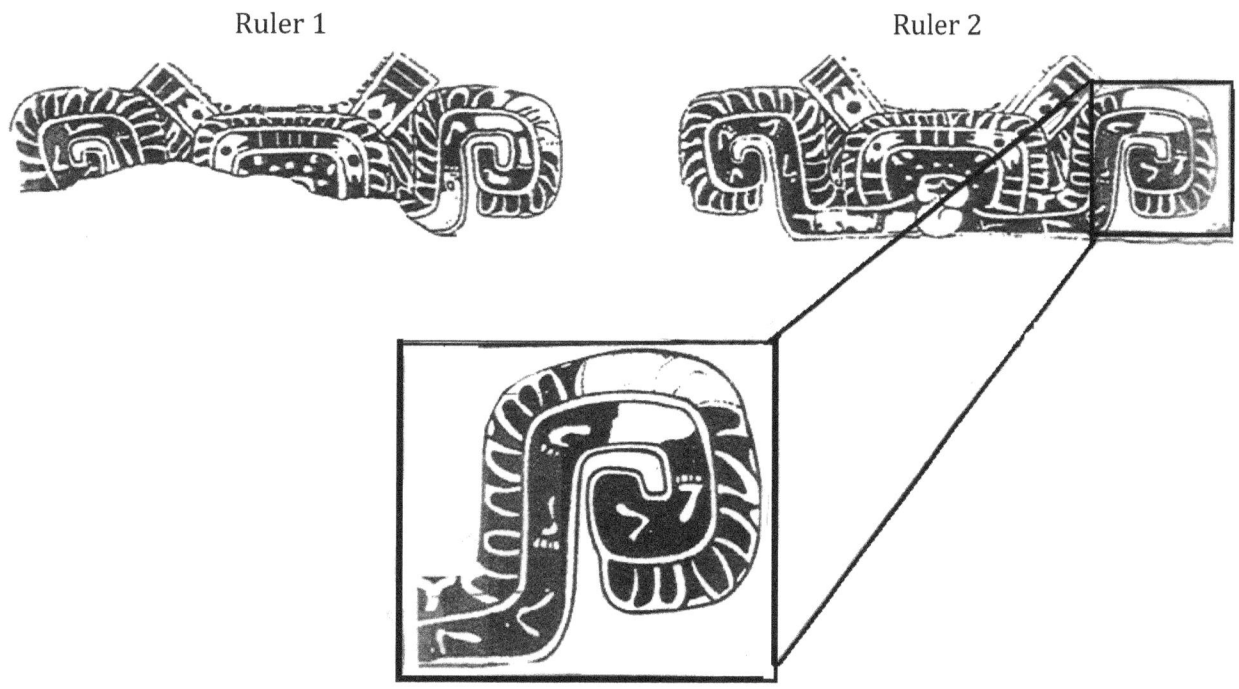

18. The glyph I call "three feather tassel" is found on its own and as part of a glyph compound. There are two occurrences where it stands on its own. In Ruler 1 and 2.

Ruler 1   Ruler 2

19. The glyph I call "object 1". It is found at P2:C1.

P2:C1

20. The glyph I call "object 2" occurs once at P2:D1.

P2:D1

21. The glyph I call "nose-plug" is found at P1:A3, P1:I1, P2:I2, P2:I4, P2:L2 and P3:C3.

P1:A3   P1:I1   P2:I2   P2:I4   P2:L2   P3:C3

22. The glyph I call "triple-mountain" has several variants: "triple-mountain" variant 1 at P2:E2, P2:H2, P3:B1, variant 2 at P2:G3, P2:K5, P3:C4, P3:H2, P3:J3, variant 3 at P2:L3, and variant 4 at P2:L4. Langley (1986) and Caso (1967) refer to this glyph similarly as "mountain triple". Von Winning (1981) observed this glyph in association with aquatic signs and has suggested that it may represent mountains covered in clouds or rain clouds at the moment of rainfall.

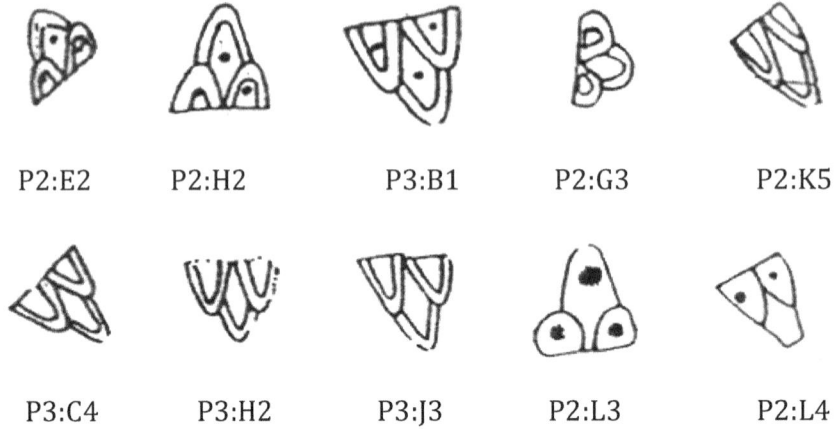

P2:E2   P2:H2   P3:B1   P2:G3   P2:K5

P3:C4   P3:H2   P3:J3   P2:L3   P2:L4

23. The glyph I call "bone" is found at P1:B2, P2:E3 and P3:F2.

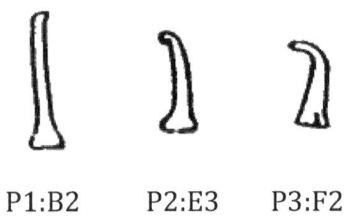

P1:B2   P2:E3   P3:F2

24. The glyph I call "object 3" occurs once at P3:G3.

P3:G3

25. This glyph I call "bird #1" appears at P2:J2.

P2:J2

26. This glyph I call "bird #2" appears once at P3:F1. This bird figure is similar to a bird figure that Pasztory (1988) identified as a "dove" from the Mythological Animals Mural at Teotihuacan.

P3:F1

27. The glyph I call "conch" appears once at P2:M2.

P2:M2

28. The glyph I call "knife" appears once at P2:F3.

P2:F3

29. The glyph I call "cacao" appears once at P3:D2.

P3:D2

30. The glyph I call "stone" appears once at P3:D4. It is similar to the Epi-Olmec "stone" glyphs.

P3:D3

31. The glyph I call "bean 1" occurs once at P3:J1.

P3:J1

32. The glyph I call "bean 2" is found at P1:B3.

P1:B3

33. This glyph I call "object 4" occurs once at P3:J2.

P3:J2

34. The glyph I call "shell" appears once at P2:I1.

P2:I1

Unreadable and partially-eroded glyphs

35. Object P1:H3, possibly "shell" or "trefoil".

    P1:H3

36. Object P2:D2

    P2:D2

37. Object P2:F2. Possibly "bean #1 or #2", "conch" or "knife".

    P2:F2

38. Object P3:H3. Possibly "flower", "shell" or "trefoil".

    P3:H3

39. Object P3:I1. Possible glyph compound containing an insect type glyph.

    P3:I1

40. Object P3:J5. Most likely "nose-plug".

    P3:J5

Glyph Compounds

41.   The first "glyph compound" is associated with Rulers 1 and 2. Although it is partially eroded in some areas in both, it appears that the partially-eroded compounds are the same as the others which are complete. The glyph compound occurs four times with each Ruler and appears to be comprised of at least six glyphic elements. I call them: "broken bundle", "reptile eye", "knot", "triangle bar", "three feather tassel" and "bundle". The glyphs I call "broken bundle" and "bundle" are after a sign that was identified as "an abstraction of the firewood bundle sign" and as representing a bundle of sticks by Von Winning (1977b in Langley 1986). Von Winning notes its similarity to the Mayan "fire" glyph T563A and suggests that like other forms of the bundle sign, it symbolizes the "binding of the years" and is used in connection with the completion of the 52-year cycle (Langley 1986: 241).

Ruler 1   Ruler 2

Glyph Compound

      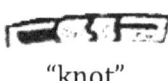

"broken bundle"   "reptile eye"   "knot"

"triangle bar"   "three-feather tassel"   "bundle"

Boundary Markers and/or Divider Glyphs

42.   The glyph I call "dot" appears randomly and numerously throughout MP. It appears to be a boundary marker or a divider.

43.   The glyph I call "bent bar" appears randomly and numerously throughout MP. It appears to be a boundary marker or a divider.

La Ventilla/Mural Painting Comparative Analysis

This comparison of the glyphs from LV and MP was carried out looking at the following criteria: 1) Are the glyphs found at LV and MP part of the same tradition? 2) Is this tradition indigenous to Teotihuacan? 3) If they are part of the same tradition, what is the overlap between them? 4) If they are not, what are the possible implications of this?

For the most part, there is very little overlap between the glyphs found at LV and those found in MP. Only several glyphs can be identified as being found in both areas. These are "reptile eye" and "three-feather tassel". The "reptile eye" glyph is wide-spread throughout Mesoamerica and thus is not exclusive to Teotihuacan or indigenous to a purely Teotihuacan tradition. The "three-feather tassel" glyph is quite common in Teotihuacan art and mural paintings and occurs in areas of the site besides LV and MP. If the LV glyphs and those from the MP were part of the same tradition, there would be substantial overlap between the two. Since there is no sizeable overlap, this suggests that the glyphs from LV and MP may not be of the same tradition. This poses other questions, such as: 1) Why was there basically no overlap between the two sets of glyphs; and 2) Are both sets indigenous to Teotihuacan, or is one set part of Teotihuacan tradition while the other is invasive?

Given the linguistic data, by Kaufman (2001b ms), that supports the idea that the base population of Teotihuacan was Totonac speaking and the elite population was Mije-Sokean speaking, one might deduce that the lack of overlap between the glyphs, if they both do in fact behave as a writing system, is a result of two different languages being spoken at the site. In spite of this, it is not likely that the Totonac speaking population (being the base population) and the Mije-Sokean speaking population (being the elite population) would employ different writing systems. From a historical standpoint, the Totonac speakers would have been subjugated by the elite Mije-Sokean speakers and, as a result, would use the Mije-Sokean writing system, if they were privy to know the script at all. Ordinarily, people use the writing system of the dominant or elite population (Kaufman 2002: pc).

Alternatively, it is possible that there was an independent Totonac speaking population, which resided outside the city of Teotihuacan, that developed its own local tradition, but it is improbable that this type of local tradition would have infiltrated the city. A reasonable conclusion therefore is that the LV style glyphs are not part of the basic tradition of Teotihuacan, and it is plausible to consider them an invasive one. Unlike the glyphs found in the MP, the LV glyphs, if not culturally found elsewhere throughout Mesoamerica (such as google-eyed-god, reptile eye, water lily), are limited to one specific area of the site. MP style glyphs are abundant and appear throughout the site in murals, on ceramics and other portable objects, and on walls. Given that the LV glyphs are clearly not coherent with those from the MP, then what is the context for the LV glyphs?

One idea could be that the glyphs from LV are actually part of the writing system of Teotihuacan, whereas the MP glyphs are a form of narrative pictography and/or visual art. LV glyphs, by contrast, are not wide-spread throughout the site, but rather are localized to one area and are more selective as to their location. In the few areas where LV style glyphs are found outside of The Plaza of the Glyphs, it is crucial to look at the context in which they occur, in addition to which glyphs they are, in order to define their possible roles as either simply part of a broader Mesoamerican iconographic tradition, visual art, or writing. When LV glyphs occur outside of the Plaza of the glyphs, they generally stand alone and rarely are positioned closely to MP style glyphs. For example, the "maguey spine and cross hatch" glyph, which is a proper LV glyph, and not found in MP, occurs elsewhere at Teotihuacan in mural paintings and other art (Fig. 31). In Figure 32, the "deer-snake" glyph appears in a mural painting and there are no easily identifiable glyphs from MP that occur in this mural. In Figure 36, the "quincross" appears at the base of the "headdress" of a "goggle-eyed" figure and no similar MP style glyphs accompany it. Figure 37 shows variants of the "flame" glyph that occur outside of LV. The "flame" glyph does not occur at MP. In Figure 37b, the "flame" glyph does not appear with MP style glyphs, but rather appears with a glyph similar to the "water lily" glyph found at LV.

Mesoamerican Day Names:

Some of the glyphs found at LV may correspond to the 20 day names of the 365-day Mesoamerican calendar. The 20 day names of the calendar are culturally specific to Mesoamerica, and therefore are identifiable in most Mesoamerican writing systems and iconography. The discovery of glyphs representing the day names accompanied by dates, or standing on their own, at Teotihuacan does not necessarily point to a full writing system. They would however provide support for one. The idea of Teotihuacan writing that included numerical coefficients that stood on their own, or with day name glyphs, has been examined in the past by a handful of scholars including: Eduard Seler (1904), Hermann Beyer (1922), Cesar Lizardi Ramos (1955), Alfonso Caso (1967), James Langley (1986) and more recently Karl Taube (2000).

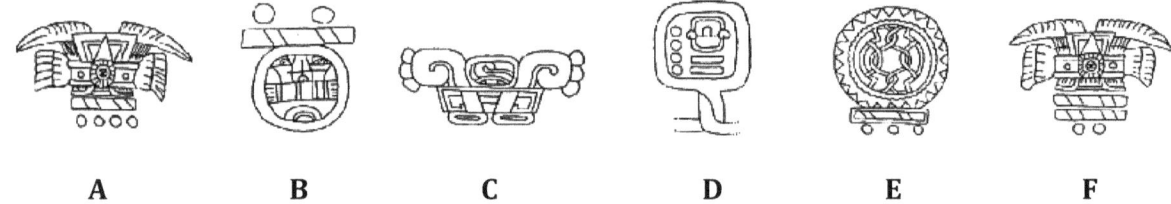

    A   **B**   **C**   **D**   **E**   **F**

Figure 44. Examples of numerical coefficients with glyphic elements at Teotihuacan (a & f) after Caso 1937: Fig. 4b&c, (b) after Caso 1937: Fig. 3, (c) after Beyer 1922: Fig. 1, (d) after Lizardi Ramos 1955: 219, (e) after Caso 1937: Fig. 9.

In previous research, the ideas of calendric elements having a presence at Teotihuacan could only be studied by analyzing Teotihuacan art, mural paintings, iconography and inscriptions or paintings on portable ceramics. The LV glyphs were not unearthed until the early 1990's and therefore provide a new body of data for consideration with reference to the 365-day Mesoamerican calendar.

Interestingly, in his 1967 work, one glyph mentioned by Caso as a probable day name is "reptile eye". The "reptile eye" glyph does have one occurrence at LV, but is also found throughout Teotihuacan, outside of the Plaza of the Glyphs, and elsewhere in Mesoamerica. It seems logical that the "reptile eye" glyph could represent one of the 20 day names in the 365-day calendar; but which? Caso asserts that the "reptile eye" glyph is the equivalent to the day *wind* in the Mesoamerican calendar, but when it is accompanied by the numeral coefficient nine, it takes on the calendric name of the god *Quetzalcoatl* (Caso 1967: 164). Caso disagrees with the interpretation by von Winning (1961), that the "reptile eye" glyph represents the day name *cayman/sea-monster* (Caso 1967: 164). Neither Caso nor von Winning interprets the "reptile eye" glyph as the day name *serpent*.

The Twenty Mesoamerican Day Names from the 365-day Calendar:

1. Cayman/Sea-monster/
2. Wind

3. Night/House/Owl
4. Iguana/Burn/Flying-turtle
5. Snake/Bad luck

6. Death/Smell

7. Deer
8. Rabbit
9. Water
10. Dog/Knot
11. Monkey

12. Twist/Tooth/Soaproot

13. Reed

14. Jaguar

15. Eagle/Maize/Farming

16. Buzzard/Crow
17. Earthquake/Long-lip/Old man

18. Flint/Victim/Cold

19. Storm/Rain/Storm-god

20. Macaw/Eye/Face

Figure 45. LV glyphs that resemble day names in other Mesoamerican writing systems and iconography. Day names in Mesoamerican systems are generally accompanied by a numeral coefficient. LV glyphs after Cabrera Castro, 1996b.

Conclusions

Much of what we know about Teotihuacan culture has come from the visual art, mural paintings and glyphs found throughout the site. The question of whether these glyphs at Teotihuacan comprise a writing system is yet to be answered completely, as there is not a sufficient body of data to work with. Although this study was not a comprehensive analysis of all glyphs at the site, the areas examined contained some of the best data available to explore with reference to a possible writing system.

From the analysis I carried out, I can assert that the glyphs from MP, in their form and in their distributions, differ from those found in most Mesoamerican writing systems. The MP glyphs were evaluated and tested in accordance with basic linguistic requirements for Mesoamerican writing systems (see Methodology). After examination, no easily identifiable calendric elements, probable personal names (although they may be unrecognizable) or year bearer signs, probable nouns or verbs were found in the MP data.

The glyphs from MP appear to be simple signs and rarely occur in compounds. The exception would be the glyph compounds that occur with the two rulers in the mural (see 41, in MP Sign Catalog). Additionally, these glyphs do not appear in any linear format. Furthermore, MP glyphs do not follow the format for most Mesoamerican writing set forth in this study (see Writing Systems). The MP glyphs were of a wide range of sizes, heights, and widths. There was no clearly identifiable reading format, layout in rows or columns, recurrent sign combinations, or identifiable order to the glyphs.

Although MP glyphs follow no clear format, which is atypical of Mesoamerican writing, there is still the possibility that they are writing. More data are necessary however to conduct further testing in this area. It is a possibility that Teotihuacan writing has its own particular style, isn't as restrictive with formatting, and differs considerably from other Mesoamerican writing systems. It is plausible that the Teotihuacanos, given their political position and power during the Classic period, established a writing system that was exclusive to them, their specific needs, and completely differed from any other writing system in use in Mesoamerica at the time.

The primary evidence to support the hypothesis that MP glyphs are much different from those found in other Mesoamerican writing systems is they are found in other parts of the site, and are numerous. Although the MP glyphs are not laid out in any comprehensible format, if a detailed study devoted solely to the MP glyphs was conducted in the future, a specific glyph pattern or a unique reading format may be identified. In my opinion, the MP glyphs are far too numerous to be filed under the category of art. I feel they must convey information, but to be certain of this, it will require a more comprehensive study as to their orientations and frequencies to identify their specific role at Teotihuacan.

The glyphs from LV show stronger evidence for being part of a probable Mesoamerican proper writing system. They may not be part of a full writing system but may be part of an incomplete writing system. Regrettably, much more data is necessary to correctly identify to which specific type of writing system they could belong. There is no clear evidence for numeral coefficients at LV. However, many of the glyphs resemble signs that serve as Day-Names of the 365-day Mesoamerican calendar in other Mesoamerican iconography and writing (when they occur with a numeral coefficient). The "deer-snake" glyph at LV, could serve as the potential day name SNAKE although it may be acceptable to other scholars to place it under DEER as well. The "deer-snake" concept is common throughout Mesoamerica referring to the boa (Kaufman: 2002, pc), and is interesting with reference to its word order. In Nawa, it is ordered *masa:kowa:tl*, or "deer-snake". Likewise, in Totonac, the order is "deer-snake", or *juukii7 luuwa7*, and in Soke, *mə 7a tzajin* or "deer-snake" (Kaufman: 2002, pc). The fact that this word is ordered "deer-snake" in all of these languages and not "snake-deer" reflects the order of linguistic elements in these languages and is quite significant. The "arrow butt" or "arrow bundle" glyphs could potentially serve as the Day-Name "REED" because reeds were the material used to make the shaft of an arrow in Mesoamerica (Kaufman 2002, pc).

LV has various occurrences of glyph compounding. The LV glyphs are all of the same basic size, height, and width. They do appear in columns and rows and three linear texts are found in the data (Fig. 46), that could possibly represent a clause, sentence or complex title. I believe the three linear texts from LV are likely to be logographic representations of three different complex titles, persons or rulers rather than clauses or sentences. LV glyphs do not seem to function within a logo-syllabic system as Zapotec, Epi-Olmec, or Mayan (Fig. 19) containing phonetic elements and syllabic signs. Rather, they appear to behave as a purely logographic system much like Xochicalco writing (Figs 26 & 47).

Figure 46. Linear texts at LV. La Ventilla glyphs after Cabrera Castro, 1996b.

"The overlord Seven Rabbit

performed a ritual four-part act of [heart]

sacrifice on captives in a temple."

Figure 47. Xochicalco Logographic Writing from the Stela Triad (Fig. 26). Interpretation after Kaufman and Justeson (1998).

Texts from Xochicalco, which date from around 800 CE, have only logograms and show no apparent phonetic component. They do, however, show Mije-Sokean word order patterns. Kaufman believes that it is most likely that at Xochicalco the elite stratum was Mije-Sokean speaking (Kaufman 2001b ms). In the absence of more data, it is impossible to present evidence for the LV glyphs as part of a logo-syllabic system because there simply are no determinable syllabic signs in the LV data. Thus, the more plausible conclusion is that they behave in a logographic system like that of Xochicalco. Assuming that the LV glyphs are a writing system, a hypothesis could be made as to their possible reading order. The LV glyphs are all leftward facing. In Mesoamerican writing systems reading order is top-to-bottom (Kaufman 2002, pc).

Also, Mesoamerican systems all function within the same reading orders depending on whether they are logo-syllabic or logographic. In logo-syllabic writing, reading order is from left to right, and in logographic writing, reading order is from right to left. Considering that LV glyphs may behave similarly to those from Xochicalco, I reviewed the Xochicalco glyphs that serve as toponyms in detail, looking for any similarities in the LV data.

Foundations of toponyms in Mixtec and Aztec iconography include: hills; a platform; a plain; a plowed field; a body of water; a current of water; a small lake/spring; a market place; a ball court; or a stone (Boone 2000: 50). With these in mind, I also compared the LV glyphs to the glyphs that serve as toponyms in Mixtec and Aztec writing and pictography as well (Fig. 15). What I found was that LV glyphs do not resemble toponyms from Xochicalco, Mixtec or Aztec writing and pictography.

At Teotihuacan, there is an enormous amount of data found throughout the site including art, iconography, and glyphic elements. Most of the glyphic elements are not presented in clear formats like other writing found elsewhere in Mesoamerica. My purpose for examining LV and MP signs was to determine if they shared traits with writing, as known elsewhere in Mesoamerica, and I found several things.

There are two sets of almost entirely non-overlapping glyph-like elements and one of these, LV, does show some of the formatting properties of writing as known elsewhere in Mesoamerica. Unfortunately, not enough of it is available to demonstrate that it spells out texts. MP does not have any identifiable formatting properties, which are required elsewhere in Mesoamerica for writing and therefore seem unpromising as a candidate for a full writing system. Hopefully in the near future more data will emerge at Teotihuacan and more scholars will take an active interest in this remarkable civilization and the possibilities that they too had a highly sophisticated way of conveying their histories through writing.

Bibliography

Acosta, Jorge R. 1964. *El Palacio del Quetzalpapalotl*. Mexico City: Instituto Nacional Antropología.

Angulo, Jorge. 2000. *Teotihuacan: City of the Gods*. Mexico City: Monclem Ediciones.

_____. 2001. Teotihuacan, aspectos de la cultura a través de su expresión pictórica. In *La pintura mural prehispánica en Mexico, Teotihuacán*. Beatriz de la Fuente edt. Vol.1, Tomo II, estudios. pp. 65-186. Mexico City: Universidad Nacional Autónoma de México.

Barthel, Thomas S. 1982. Varitable "Texts" in Teotihuacan Art? *The Masterkey* 56(I): 4-11. Los Angeles: The Southwest Museum Los Angeles.

Benson, Elizabeth P., edt. 1973. *MesoAmerican Writing Systems*. Washington, D.C.: Dumbarton Oaks.

Berdan, Frances F. and Anawalt, Patricia Rieff. 1997. *The Essential Codex Mendoza*. Berkley and Los Angeles: University of California Press.

Berlo, Janet Catherine, Editor. 1988. *Art, Ideology, and the city of Teotihuacan*. Washington, D.C.: Dumbarton Oaks.

_____. 1983. Conceptual Categories for the Study of Texts and Images in Mesoamerica. In *Text and Image in Pre-Columbian Art* (Janet C. Berlow ed.): 1-39. BAR International Series 180, Oxford.

_____. 1989. Early Writing in Central Mexico: in tlilli, in tlapalli before A.D.1000 In *MesoAmerica After the Decline of Teotihuacan, A.D. 700–900*, ed. Richard A. Diehl and Janet Catherine Berlo, 19-47. Washington, D.C.: Dumbarton Oaks.

Berrin, Kathleen, and Millon, Clara *et al.* 1988. *Feathered Serpents and Flowering Trees: Reconstructing the Murals of Teotihuacan*. Seattle: University of Washington Press.

Berrin, Kathleen, and Pasztory, Esther, eds. 1993. *Teotihuacan: Art from the City of the Gods*. New York: Thames and Hudson.

Beyer, Hermann. 1921. Algo sobre los signos chinos de Teotihuacan. *El Mexico Antiguo* 1: 211. Mexico.

_____. 1922. Sobre una plaqueta con una deidad Teotihuacana. *Memorias, Sociedad Cientifica Antonio Alzate* 40: 549-58. Mexico.

Bone, Lesley. 1986. "Teotihuacan Mural Project" in WAAC Newsletter. Vol. 8, Number 3. pp. 2-7.

Boone, Elizabeth Hill. 1994. Writing and Recording Knowledge. In *Writing Without Words: Alternative Literacies in MesoAmerica and the Andes*, edited by Elizabeth H. Boone and Walter D. Mignolo, pp. 3-26. Durham: Duke University Press.

_____. ed. 1999. *Collecting The Pre-Columbian Past*. Washington, D.C.: Dumbarton Oaks.

_____. 2000. *Stories in Red and Black: Pictoral Histories of the Aztecs and Mixtecs*. Austin: University of Texas Press.

Boone, Elizabeth, edt. and Benson, Elizabeth P., org. 1982. *The Art and Iconography of Late Post-Classic Central Mexico*. Washington, D.C.: Dumbarton Oaks.

Boone, Elizabeth Hill, and Mignolo, Walter D. 1996. *Writing Without Words: Alternative Literacies in MesoAmerica and the Andes*. Durham: Duke University Press.

Braun, Barbara. 1982. Subtle Diplomacy Solves a Custody Case. *Art News* 81 (6): 100-103.

Brotherson, Gordon. 1995. *Painted Books from Mexico*. London: British Museum Press.

Cabrera Castro, Ruben. 1996a. Caracteres glíficos Teotihuacanos en un piso de La Ventilla. In *La pintura mural prehispánica en México, Teotihuacán*, edited by Beatriz de la Fuente, vol. 1, tomo 2, pp. 400-27. Mexico City: Universidad Nacional Autónoma de México.

_____. 1996b. Figuras glíficas de La Ventilla, Teotihuacan. *Arqueología* 15:27-40.

Carmack, Robert M., Gasco, Janine, and Gossen, Gary H. 1996. *The Legacy of Mesoamerica: History and Culture of a Native American Civilization*. Uppersaddle River: Prentice Hall.

Carrasco, David. 1990. *Religions of Mesoamerica*. Prospect Heights: Waveland Press, Inc.

_____. 1999. *City of Sacrifice*. Boston: Beacon Press.

_____. 2000. *MesoAmericas Classic Herritage*. Boulder: University Press of Colorado.

_____. (edt.) 2001. *The Oxford Encyclopedia of Mesoamerican Cultures, The civilizations of Mexico and Central America*. Oxford: Oxford University Press.

Caso, Alfonso. 1937. ¿Tenían los Teotihuacanos conocimiento del tonalpohualli? *El México Antiguo* 4(3-4): 131-143.

_____. 1960. *Interpretación del Códice Bodley 2858*. Accompanied by a facsimile of the Codex. Mexico City: Sociedad Mexicana de Antropología.

_____. 1964. *Interpretación del Códice Selden 3135* (A.2). Accompanied by a facsimile of the Codex. Mexico City: Sociedad Mexicana de Antropología.

_____. 1967. *Los calendarios prehispanicos*. Mexico City: Universidad Nacional Autónoma de México.

Chadwick, Robert E. L. 2013. *The Olmeca-Xicalanca of Teotihuacan, Cacaxtla and Cholula. An archaeological, ethnohistorical and linguistic synthesis*. With a contribution of Angel Garcia Cook: El Epiclásico en la región poblano-tlaxcalteca: BAR International Series 2488. Oxford.

Cobean, Robert H. 2013. Tula. Fondo de Cultura Económica.

Coe, Michael D. 1962. *Mexico: From the Olmecs to the Aztecs*. New York: Thames and Hudson.

Cowgill, George L. 1992. Teotihuacan Glyphs and Imagery in the light of Some Early Colonial Texts. *In Art, Ideology and the City of Teotihuacan*. Edited by Janet Catherine Berlo, pp 231-246. Washington, D.C.: Dumbarton Oaks.

_____. 1997. State and Society at Teotihuacan, Mexico. In *Annual Review of Anthropology*, volume 26, edited by William H. Durham, pp. 129-161. Annual Reviews Inc., Palo Alto.

DeFrancis, John. 1989. *Visible Speech: The Diverse Oneness of Writing Systems*. Honolulu: University of Hawaii Press.

de La Fuente, Beatriz, edt. 1995. *La pintura mural prehispánica en México, Teotihuacán*. Mexico D.F.: UNAM, Instituto de Investigaciones Esteticas.

Diaz, Gisele, and Rodgers, Alan. 1993. *The Codex Borgia*. New York: Dover Publications, Inc.

Dibble, Charles E., ed. 1951. *Códice Xolotl*. Mexico City: Universidad Nacional Autónoma de México and the University of Utah.

_____. 1980. 2 vols. *Códice Xolotl*. Mexico City: Universidad Nacional Autónoma de México.

Diehl, Richard A. and Berlo, Janet Catherine. 1989. *MesoAmerica after the Decline of Teotihuacan A.D. 700–900*. Washington, D.C: Dumbarton Oaks Research Library and Collection.

Evans, Susan T. and Berlo, Janet Catherine. 1992. Teotihuacan: An Introduction. *In Art, Ideology, and the City of Teotihuacan*, 1-26. Washington, D.C.: Dumbarton Oaks.

Galarza, Joaquín and Libura, Krystyna M. 1999. *La tira de la peregrinación: para leer*. Mexico D.F.: Ediciones Tecolote.

Gelb, I. J. 1963. *A Study of Writing*. Chicago: University of Chicago.

_____. 1973. Written Records and Decipherment. In *Current Trends in Linguistics*, edited by Thomas A. Sebeok. Vol. 11, *Diachronic, Areal, and Typological Linguistics*. Paris: Mouton.

Gendrop, Paul. 1984. *El Tablero-talud y otros perfiles arquitectonicos en Msoamerica. Cuadernos de arquitectura mesoamericana 2*, Mexico City: UNAM, division de Estudios posgrado, facultad de arquitectura.

Grove, David C. and Joyce, Rosemary A., edts. 1999. *Social Patterns in Pre-Classic MesoAmerica*. Washington, D.C.: Dumbarton Oaks.

Harris, John F and Stearns, Stephen K. 1997. *Understanding Maya Inscriptions*. Philadelphia: University of Pennsylvania Press.

Hassig, Ross. 1945. *Trade, Tribute, and Transportation*. Norman: University of Oklahoma Press.

Heyden, Doris. 1998. *Mexico: Origines de un simbolo*. Mexico City: CNCA. Joralemon, P. David. 1971. A study of Olmec iconography. Studies in Pre-Columbian Art and Architecture, no.7. Washington, D.C.: Dumbarton Oaks.

Hirth, Ken. 2000. *Ancient Urbanism at Xochicalco. The Evolution and Organization of a Prehispanic Society*. Volumes 1 and 2. The University of Utah Press, Salt Lake City.

Joralemon, P. David. 1971. *A study of Olmec iconography*. Studies in Pre-Columbian Art and Architecture, no.7. Washington, D.C.: Dumbarton Oaks.

Justeson, John and Kaufman, Terrence. 1993. A Decipherment of Epi-Olmec Hieroglyphic Writing. In *Science* vol. 259, pp. 1703-1711.

_____. 1997. A Newly Discovered Column in the Hieroglyphic Text on the La Mojarra Stela 1: A Test of the Epi-Olmec Decipherment. In *Science* vol. 277, pp. 207-210.

Kaufman, Terrence. 1963 ms. Mije-Soke Diachronic Studies.

_____. 1994. The Native Languages of Mesoamerica in Atlas of the World's Languages (Routledge Reference) edited by R.E. Asher and Christopher Moseley. New York: Routledge.

_____. 2001a ms. The History of the Nawa Language Group From the Earliest Times to the Sixteenth Century: Some Initial Results.

_____. 2001b ms. Language History and Language Contact in Pre-Classic Meso-America, with Special Focus on the Language of Teotihuacan.

Kaufman, Terrence and Justeson, John. 1998 ms. The Stela Texts at Xochicalco: Chronology, Parsing, and Semantics.

_____. 2001 ms. Zapotec Hieroglyphic Writing.

_____. 2002 ms. The Decipherment of Zapotec Hieroglyphic Writing.

Kirchoff, Paul. 1943. Mesoamérica, sus límites geográficos, composición étnica, y carectares culturales. *Acta Americana* 1. 97-107.

Kubler, George. 1967. *The Iconography of the Art of Teotihuacan*. Studies in Pre-Columbian Art and Archaeology, no. 4. Washington, D.C.: Dumbarton Oaks.

Langley, James C. 1986. *Symbolic Notation of Teotihuacan: Elements of Writing in a Mesoamerican Culture of the Classic period*. BAR International Series 313. Oxford.

_____. 1992. Teotihuacan Sign Clusters: Emblem or Articulation? *In Art, Ideology, and the City of Teotihuacan*, edited by Janet C. Berlo, pp. 247-80. Washington, D.C: Dumbarton Oaks.

_____. 1993. Symbols, Signs, and Writing Systems. In *Teotihuacan: Art From the City of the Gods*. Edited by Kathleen Berrin and Esther Pasztory, pp 128-139. London and New York: Thames & Hudson.

Lizardi Ramos, Cesar. 1955. ¿Conocían el xihuitl los Teotihuacanos? *El Mexico Antiguo* 8:219-23. Mexico.

Lopez Luján, Leonardo. 1989. *La recuperacion mexica del pasado Teotihuacano, Proyecto Templo Mayor*. Mexico City: INAH.

Macri, Martha J and Stark, Laura M. 1993. *A Sign Catalog of the La Mojarra Script*. San Francisco: Pre-Columbian Art Research Institute.

Macri, Martha and Ford, Anabel, editors. 1997. *The Language of Maya Hieroglyphs*. San Francisco:Pre-Columbian Art Research Institute.

Malmstrom, Vincent H. 1997. *Cycles of the Sun, Mysteries of the Moon*. Austin: University of Texas Press.

Mendoza, Ruben G. 2001. *Mesomerican Chronology* in The Oxford Encyclopedia of Mesoamerican Cultures, The civilizations of Mexico and Central America, pp. 222-226) Oxford: Oxford University Press.

Miller, Arthur G. 1973. *The Mural Paintings of Teotihuacan*. Washington, D.C.: Dumbarton Oaks.

Miller, Mary Ellen. 1986. *The Art of Mesoamerica*. New York: Thames and Hudson.

Miller, Mary and Karl Taube. 1993. *An Illustrated Dictionary of the Gods and Symbols of Mesoamerica*. New York: Thames and Hudson.

Millon, Clara. 1973. Painting, Writing, and Polity in Teotihuacan, Mexico. *American Antiquity* 38 (3): 294-314.

Noguez, Xavier, ed. 1978. *Tira de Tepechpan: Códice colonial procedente del valle de México*. 2 vols. Mexico City: Biblioteca Enciclopédica del Estado de México.

Panofsky, Erwin. 1939. *Studies in Iconology*. Oxford: Oxford University Press.

Pasztory, Esther. 1974. *The Iconography of the Teotihuacan Tlaloc*. Studies in Pre-Columbian Art and Archaeollgy, 15. Washington D.C.: Dumbarton Oaks.

_____. 1998. *Pre-Columbian Art*. Cambridge: Cambridge University Press.

_____. 1997. *Teotihuacan: An Experiment in Living*. Norman: University of Oklahoma Press.

Pohl, John M.D. 1999. *Exploring MesoAmerica*. Oxford: Oxford University Press.

Reid, Aileen A., Ruth G Bishop, Ella M. Button, and Robert E. Longacre. 1968. *Totonac: From Clause to Discourse*. Norman: University of Oklahoma.

_____. 1991. *Gramática Totonaca de Xicotepec de Juárez, Puebla*. Mexico City: The Summer Institute of Linguistics.

Sabloff, Jeremy A. 1989. *The Cities of Ancient Mexico: Reconstructing a Lost World*. New York: Thames and Hudson.

Saenz, Cesar. 1961. Tres estelas en Xochicalco. *Revista Mexicana de Estudios Antropológicos* 17: 39-65.

Sahagún, Fray Bernardino de. 1950-1982. *Florentine Codex: General History of the Things of New Spain*. Translated and edited by Arthur J. O. Anderson and Charles E. Dibble. Monographs of the School of American Research 14, pts. 2-13. Salt Lake City: University of Utah Press. (Originally written 1575-1577 or 1578-1580.)

Schele, Linda and Grube Nikolaï. 2002. *Introduction to Reading Maya Hieroglyphs*. For the 26th Maya Hieroglyphic Forum at Texas. Maya Workshop Foundation.

Sejourne, Laurette. 1956. *Burning Water, Thought and Religion in Ancient Mexico*. New York.

_____. 1959. *Un palacio en la ciudad de los dioses (Teotihuacan)*. INAH, Mexico.

_____. 1966. *Arqueologia de Teotihuacán, la ceramica*. Mexico.

Seler, Eduard. 1904. *Mexican Picture Writing of Alexander von Humbolt*, Bureau of Amer. Ethnol. Bull. 28. Washingon.

Shook, Edwin M. and Robert F. Heizer. 1976. An Olmec Sculpture From the South (Pacific) Coast of Guatemala. *Journal of New World Archaeology*, 1:3 Los Angeles.

Sosa, Constanza Vega, cord. 2000. *Codices y Documentos sobre Mexico, Tercer Simposio Internacional*. Mexico City: INAH.

Taube, Karl. 1992. The Iconography of Mirrors at Teotihuacan. In *Art, Ideology, and the City of Teotihuacan*, edited by Janet C. Berlo, pp. 169-204. Washington, D.C.: Dumbarton Oaks.

_____. 1993. *Aztec & Maya Myths*. Austin: University of Texas Press.

_____. 1999. The Turquoise Hearth: Fire, Sacrifice, and the Central Mexican Cult of War. In *MesoAmerica's Classic Heritage: From Teotihuacan to the Great Aztec Temple*, edited by David Carrasco, Lindsay Jones, and Scott Sessions. Niwot: University Press of Colorado.

_____. 2000. *Ancient America: Writing System of Teotihuacan*. Washington, D.C.: Center for Ancient American Studies.

Taylor, Isaac. 1899. *The History of the Alphabet*. 2 vols. New York: Schribner's.

Urcid, Javier. 2001. *Zapotec Hieroglyphic Writing*. Studies in Pre-Columbian Art & Archaeology, no. 34. Washington D.C., Dumbarton Oaks.

Vogel, Susana. 1995. *Teotihuacan: Historia, Arte Y Monumentos.* Mexico City: Monclem Ediciones, S.A. de C.V.

von Winning, Hasso. 1949. Shell Designs on Teotihuacan pottery. *El México Antiguo*, vol. VII, pp. 126-153.

_____. 1961. Teotihuacan Symbols: The Reptile's Eye Glyph. *Ethos*, vol. 26, no.3. Stockholm.

_____. 1981. La iconogafía de Teotihuacan: los dioses y los signos. 2 vols. Mexico, D.F: Universidad Nacional Autónoma de México

_____. 1987. *La iconogafía de Teotihuacan: los dioses y los signos,* tomo I y II. Mexico City: Universidad Nacional Autónoma de México.

Wauchope, Robert, ed. 1975. *Handbook of Middle American Indians*, volume 15. Austin: University of Texas Press.

Wichmann, Soren. 1995. *The Relationship Among the Mixe-Zoquean Languages of Mexico.* Salt Lake City: University of Utah Press.

www.ingramcontent.com/pod-product-compliance
Lightning Source LLC
Chambersburg PA
CBHW041709290426
44108CB00027B/2907